Sir Charles Tupper: Warhorse

Prime Ministers of Canada

by Paula Johanson

CHARLES TUPPER: WARHORSE

First edition. January 24, 2021.

Copyright © 2021 Paula Johanson.

ISBN: 978-1989966143

Written by Paula Johanson.

For Gavin, Dexter, and Alice

my little pals from Nova Scotia

"I am a Canadian,
free to speak without fear,
free to worship in my own way,
free to stand for what I think right,
free to oppose what I believe wrong,
or free to choose those who shall govern my country.
This heritage of freedom
I pledge to uphold
for myself and all mankind."
From the Canadian Bill of Rights,
July 1, 1960.

———————— ⟨∾⟩ ————————

"We are not the country we thought we were.
History will be re-written. We are all accountable."
Gord Downie, 2016

Introduction

IN SCHOOL, WE'RE TAUGHT to think of Canadian history as calm, and resolutely proceeding towards an obvious goal. With no big War of Independence or Civil War, it seems like the Confederation of Canada just simply happened. And the Fathers of Confederation look in their photos like sober, serious men who reached a sensible agreement after some quiet talk.

HAH! At least one of those Fathers of Confederation was an aggressive, opinionated loudmouth. Charles Tupper argued at three conferences, while each region was protecting their own agendas. Among those delegates, Alexander Tilloch Galt was a diplomat, working for compromise. Thomas D'Arcy McGee was a poet and a revolutionary whose active tongue got him assassinated a few years later. Two Québécois were careful to use English among all these Anglophones. John A. Macdonald worked as an enabler, the human lubricant in these machinations, and emerged as the first prime minister for Confederation. But it was the rhetoric of Charles Tupper that brought the conference delegates together, exhausting their disagreements and insisting to each that their regions would be better served as a province of Confederation.

Charles Tupper was a man of many talents. Each of his occupations was a career in its own right. He was a doctor first, and a medical administrator. He became a newspaper editor and businessman. When called on by the Conservatives, he became a politician. Later as a High Commissioner, he put all his talents to work representing Canada's interests in Britain.

Historians have called him "a large and attractive man," but flattery aside, he was a bully. He wasn't above using his physical presence to dominate others, in a time when working men tended to be tough but small from poor nutrition, and men trained to office work were not muscular. "In the Commons, Tupper was known for speeches that may have lacked grace, but were full of thunder."[1]

As a favourite colleague of Macdonald, he was busy in six different cabinet roles over the years, but did not become prime minister until every other alternative had been exhausted.

They called him the War Horse of Cumberland County. Charles Tupper met every challenge that came his way. He didn't always win, but that wasn't for lack of trying. He tried to keep his personal history anecdotal. If it's not in a document, it can't be referenced; if it can't be brought to the attention of an authority, it didn't count. And if he brought it to attention, he wanted it noticed.

As a boy, he set goals, and learned to test his abilities. As a young medical student, he strove to learn the mysteries of how bones and muscles worked, but also took thought for the feelings and beliefs of people under his care.

That he was a brave man, no one questioned. He also sang his own praises shamelessly. While at college, he went out on thin ice to save a drowning man. He was a country doctor, dedicated to saving lives, even when it meant handling patients with cholera or tuberculosis in a time when there were no miracle cures for these illnesses. When word came that his grown daughter was in a dangerous situation, he travelled over 2,000 kilometres from Ottawa to the Red River Valley to bring her home. Trains and carts did not cover the entire route, and it was on foot and by sled that he made the last parts of the journey.

Becoming a politician did not put an end to his medical practise. Even after becoming premier of Nova Scotia, he was still the chief medical officer at Halifax, and chief surgeon at Nova Scotia's provincial hospital. He was the first medical doctor to become premier of Nova Scotia, and the only physician ever to be a prime minister of Canada. Under his seat in the Legislature, and in Parliament, was a medical bag.

Everyone who met him had strong opinions about Charles Tupper. The people whose lives he saved knew him to be a dedicated doctor who braved epidemics and would travel dozens of miles by driving a wagon or riding horses to treat his patients. The people who served with him in government and on committees knew him to be opinionated to the point of arrogance and even a bully. The strength of his personality was put to use, and not only when speaking out for his beliefs. He was rumoured to be a ladies' man with many conquests. He was also a skilled mediator who could get people to work together, even when they were on opposing sides of an issue.

"He was one of those people," wrote historian Craig Brown, "who believe you can carry anything through if you have enough brass." His assertive style veered into aggressive behaviour, earning him as many opponents as friends. He worked to benefit his people, which expanded over time from his family and patients to include his county, Nova Scotia, and Canada. Unfortunately, he didn't extend this same sense of responsibility to the First Nations. As Canada grew to include the west, he always worked in support of Canada, rather than the interests of First Nations people, or Britain, or the United States.

For forty-one years Sir Charles Tupper served in politics, before he became the prime minister of Canada. The position was to be his for ten weeks. He did not become the prime minister by leading his party into an election and winning a majority of seats in the House of Commons. Instead, he was the fourth of four prime ministers who served out the end of a term when the position was empty after Sir John A. Macdonald's death. As prime minister, Tupper served in office for only sixty-nine days. It was the shortest term yet served by any Canadian prime minister, and the entire term took place during an election campaign. Though during previous elections Tupper had been elected as a Member of Parliament, he never won election as a prime minister. Nineteen years after that lost election and almost on his deathbed, the Old Warhorse was still an influence on prime minister Robert Borden who was then in office.

1 Azzi, Stephen. "Election of 1896." Historica Canada. Revised September 2, 2015. http://www.thecanadianencyclopedia.ca/en/article/election-1896-feature/

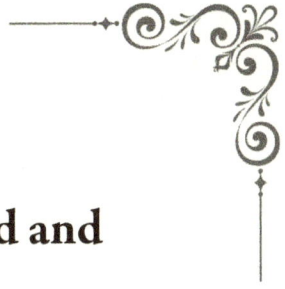

Chapter 1: Background and Youth

CHARLES TUPPER WAS born in Nova Scotia, a colony that had been founded as Acadia in 1605 by the French, and conquered by the British in 1710. The Mi'kmaq, a First Nations people who have lived there since time immemorial, were crowded aside by the growing population of English-speaking colonists. By 1758, the colony of Nova Scotia had established representative government and held a Burying the Hatchet ceremony, ending war with the Mi'kmaq. As United Empire Loyalists migrated from the new American states after the American Revolution, the British colony expanded into areas that were later separated into the colonies of Prince Edward Island and New Brunswick and Cape Breton. Among these United Empire Loyalists was the Tupper family; there were members who had fought on both sides of the battle at Bunker Hill. Among those extended family members who remained in the new American states were some who a hundred years later would be found on both sides of the American Civil War.

A Growing Family

The parents of the boy who would grow up to be Sir Charles Tupper were a couple who met and married near Amherst, Nova Scotia. The Reverend Charles Tupper worked as a school principal and a Baptist preacher. As well, he wrote for a number of magazines and newspapers. The scholarly Reverend understood thirteen languages, and was able to read the Bible in Greek, Latin, Hebrew, and Syriac, as well as the Romance languages Italian, Spanish, Portuguese and German.

When the bachelor Reverend Charles married the widow Miriam Lockhart (neé Lowe), he became an instant stepfather to her six young children. Though she was physically delicate, Miriam had survived while her first husband had died of consumption, a name then used for tuberculosis. Only 26 years old, Miriam was shy in spite of her intelligence. Her Bible knowledge and religious devotion made her an appealing wife for her new minister husband.

Both the Reverend Charles and Miriam were of Planter stock – that is, descended from settlers from the New England colonies who had responded to invitations from the governor of Nova Scotia to settle lands left vacant in 1755 after the Acadian Expulsion. Their ancestors were Puritans who came to Nova Scotia from Connecticut. Together, Miriam and the Reverend Charles had five more children, though one died as an infant. The second of the children of their union was Charles, born on July 2, 1821.

Their home on a small farm was not a mansion, but it was filled with books on art and literature as well as religion. Homeschooling was the family education choice at first, and it worked well to prepare the children for later schooling. By the age of seven, young Charles had read the entire Bible aloud to his father during their study sessions. Other forms of learning were shared, particularly music lessons for the children. As well, to help him find his way at night if he ever got lost, young Charles was taught about the stars by his father. He was shown by the age of nine how to find the North Star and use it to choose his direction, and how to be aware of the passing of time through the night as stars wheeled 'round the North Star.

Both parents believed that studying another language would strengthen the brain – a belief that over a hundred and fifty years later would be verified with neurological studies. Young Charles benefited from his parents' interest in language studies. While Charles studied at home, his father taught him to translate Latin into English, and as a motivator would pay him a halfpenny for every page of translation that he could complete. A bright boy, young Charles could learn quickly. He became confident that he could accomplish anything with learning and hard work, and this confidence made him seem arrogant.

Epidemics

Though Charles' mother was well-educated with Bible study and languages, she gave an entirely different kind of education to her son as well as access to her books. Miriam taught him by example how to care for the illnesses of family and neighbours.

In 1830, all the Tupper children came down with a sickness called "scarlatina with putrid sore throat." Scarlet fever usually starts as a throat infection with what is recognised today as Streptococcus A bacteria. Fever and sore throat progress to chills, vomiting, abdominal pain, and malaise. The rash and peeling skin are uncomfortable. With no antibiotics available at that time, the only medical treatment was painkillers, rest, and plenty of clean fluids to drink. Without this care, a person could easily die.

Miriam Tupper, a slim woman of delicate build, nursed all her children back to health. As wife to Reverend Tupper, she was familiar to many of their neighbours. Throughout the scarlatina epidemic, she visited the sick people in their homes, bathing them and feeding them by hand until they were able to look after themselves. In the way that a public-health nurse does today, Miriam Tupper cared for people in her community, treating their illnesses and helping them learn how to improve their health.

It was an important lesson for young Charles, that caring for others was more than an idea – it was a practical thing which could have such positive results. He realised that his delicate mother could face the dangers of this epidemic and not fall ill because of her clean habits and good health.

During the 1800s, epidemics of contagious diseases were common in Canada. These illnesses included diphtheria, smallpox, typhus, typhoid, cholera, polio, and "fever and ague" or tertiary fever, later called malaria. The fevers caused by these diseases were particularly devastating to First Nations people. Tuberculosis, or "consumption" as it was known then, was common among any people, especially those with inadequate nutrition or housing. As each group of immigrants arrived from overseas, new illnesses came as well, making them and others fall ill. Measles, mumps, and rubella weren't considered simple childhood diseases; these are life-threatening illnesses for people who don't have access to medical care. All these diseases have become rare in Canada during the 21st century because of vaccination, medical care, and food safety, none of which were commonly available when Charles was growing up in the colony of Nova Scotia. Young Charles never forgot seeing how much difference could be made by simple good care for common illnesses.

A Day's Adventure

One day. twelve-year-old Charles and his younger brother Nathan, then ten years old, found a log that had been hollowed out into a canoe. They rigged up a sail and launched their rough boat into a creek. A sudden gust of wind, and Charles' lurching reaction, sent the boat over and both boys fell into the rushing water.

Unfortunately, neither knew how to swim! It took a great deal of thrashing to get them both safely to shore. Their clothes were soaking wet, but dried after a while in the sunshine and wind. The boys dressed and slunk back home, hoping their mother wouldn't notice and ask questions about what they had been doing.

This story might horrify urban parents in the 21st century who drive their twelve-year-olds to and from soccer practice, but it's not an unreasonable event. Charles grew up in a time without playgrounds, Boy Scouts, or soccer leagues. Even today, many children growing up in rural homes will make their own fun in ways that can be as challenging as this improvised canoe.

Medical Education

In August of 1836, Charles began a medical apprenticeship with Dr Benjamin Page in Amherst. For a fifteen-year-old boy in the 19th century, many kinds of apprenticeship involved the same duties, no matter what the discipline. He spent each working day in the company of his master, carrying his tools and gear when they had to travel by foot or wagon. He would have a modest bed and board at his master's home. He would keep their workplace tidy, haul water by pails full each day, and keep the firewood chopped or coal bin filled to heat the stove. All the tedious work of grinding medicinal ingredients with a mortar and pestle was his duty, and any heavy lifting as well. The medical part of his training included directed reading with the doctor, and observation while assisting the doctor with patients. Germ theory was in its infancy and not widely accepted, but hygiene and sanitation were understood to be essential for personal and public health.

A year or so as apprentice was all the training many healers ever had at that time, but Charles was interested in becoming a real physician with the best training he could get. He began by spending the year of 1837 at Horton Academy in Wolfville, Nova Scotia, studying Latin, Greek, French, and the sciences. Charles picked up some wrestling moves as well, in the gymnasium. By working at odd jobs and teaching, he was able to earn some money. Mathematics was a more difficult challenge for him. When Charles couldn't solve some math problems his teacher had assigned, he turned to the principal for help. After several tries, the principal admitted that he was unable to solve the problems either. That was enough for Charles. He quit working on the problems, reasoning that surely the school would not require him to know any more than the principal did. Of course, he got a bad mark in mathematics.

For a proper medical education, he would have to travel to Scotland for a four-year degree in medicine. He could reduce the time by a year if he apprenticed with a more well-known and reputable physician. That would make the expense of education more affordable. In 1839, he taught in a simple school for a few months to earn a little money, then began a second apprenticeship with Dr Ebenezer Fitch Harding in Windsor, Nova Scotia. This ten months of work was the making of him as a physician, surgeon, and apothecary (pharmacist). At eighteen years old, Charles worked day and night with Dr Harding to prepare medicines, deliver babies, and tend those who were ill.

One afternoon, he observed as Dr Harding and a colleague amputated the leg of a First Nations patient. Harding gave the leg to Charles to dissect as a practical lesson in anatomy. It is essential for a medical student learning surgery to do dissections, to understand how bones and muscles work together. Before he could begin, the relatives of the patient spoke to him; perhaps they found a young apprentice to be more approachable than an older doctor. According to their beliefs, unless the leg was buried in sacred ground, in the afterlife the patient would be unable to walk. Touched by their concerns and trust, Charles promised to respect their beliefs. When he finished studying the amputated leg, he found a small wooden box to hold it. As he later told the story in his memoir, after dark that night, he carried the box under his cloak to the Roman Catholic graveyard. Secretly, he buried it there, to honour his promise. Perhaps he felt unable to approach the local priest with his story.

The letter of recommendation Dr Harding wrote for him was exactly what he needed to be accepted at the University of Edinburgh. "I am highly satisfied with his abilities, correct moral deportment, and with the zeal and diligence he has manifested in the prosecution of the various studies connected with the profession of medicine," wrote Harding.

A Sea Journey

In August 1840, nineteen-year-old Charles left Windsor for Scotland. It was a six-week journey – a long time away from fresh meat or vegetables. This was no holiday on a passenger ship. On the brigantine Huntington, there was so much lumber loaded that planks were stacked on the deck as high as the railings. Charles was one of two passengers, along with the ship's captain, mate, and three crew members. He was seasick most of the time.

Seasickness may have been why he felt ill from the smoke of the mate's pipe. The mate saw no reason to move downwind, and though Charles asked him to put it out, the mate refused. Charles threw the first punch in their fight, breaking the pipe into pieces against the man's jaw. The mate grabbed for Charles, who when telling the story in later years insisted he managed to put to good use some wrestling moves that he learned at Horton Academy. They had to be separated by a crew member who had been steering the ship. The ship was drifting off course by the time the captain arrived. The mate was confined to his bunk for the next three days, and made a point of never blowing smoke again into that passenger's face.

When the ship docked at Glasgow harbour, Charles found his equilibrium again on land. He caught the stagecoach to Edinburgh, where he enrolled in the University. Exactly how he managed to afford the expense of tuition and travel, as well as room and board, is a bit mysterious; there are rumours he was partially funded by an affectionate lady of means, but he did not marry her on his return to Nova Scotia.

On Thin Ice

While studying in Edinburgh, each winter Charles enjoyed a few weeks of skating on Duddiston Loch. This sheltered body of water is about half a mile long (less than a kilometre) and two hundred yards wide (almost two hundred metres). One afternoon, there was a warning posted about thin ice. He heard a commotion across the loch, where several people were in the water.

"I skated directly across the loch with the ice waving under my feet like a sheet," he wrote later in his journal. Rescuers were helping some of the skaters, and he went to the one who was drowning. The ice broke beneath him as well. When an iceboat was pulled to the hole, he helped the other man out and all were taken safely to shore. That evening, when he entered a lecture hall, his fellow students applauded his bravery. He admitted later in his journal: "It was not courage, but an impulse I could not resist. A thousand pounds would not have tempted me to skate across the loch before or after that event. My anxiety to escape recognition was to prevent my name getting in the papers and the shock it would give my mother, who was an invalid, when she heard of it."[1]

There are few other anecdotes to tell from his time as a medical student, except for a pair of interesting facts. He was regarded as a good "saw man," because he was bigger than many surgeons, with the upper body strength to perform an amputation promptly with fewer saw strokes. As well, before he was twenty-two years old, Tupper had already assisted at 116 births.[2]

Demon Rum

Raised as a Christian by his parents, young Charles attended the Baptist church where his father was a co-pastor. Religion began to matter more to him personally while apprenticed to Dr Harding, as Charles had a conversion experience. That's understandable for a very young man facing medical challenges of births and deaths.

Then during his medical studies in Edinburgh, he was introduced to a world of temptations which had not been available to him in Amherst: theatre, restaurants or public houses, and alcohol. (His colonial upbringing must have been spartan indeed if Edinburgh was a cosmopolitan challenge.) It comes as no surprise that Charles gave in to such temptations, and gave up the Baptist prejudice against them. It is likely that he danced with ladies, and possible that he might even have played cards – both were shocking ideas for many Baptists even a hundred years later.

Charles also took the opportunity to try drinking alcohol. As could be expected for the son of a Baptist pastor, he had no experience yet to teach him to drink in moderation. His father was horrified to learn he fell victim to the demon rum, and exclaimed aloud in disbelief, "Is it possible?" Charles was lucky to escape being thrashed with a horsewhip, as some other fathers of that time did to punish their sons. His father preferred to model the merits of hard work and self-discipline. Maybe the good example paid off, but when this young inconsistent Baptist did try drinking Scotch whiskey in Edinburgh, he learned to drink socially and in moderation, or something approaching moderation. In years to come when Tupper became a friend and colleague of Sir John A. Macdonald, he did not drink hard liquor to frequent excess as Macdonald did.

1 Saunders, E.M., editor. The Life and Letters of the Rt. Hon. Sir Charles Tupper, Bart., K.C.M.G. Toronto, ON: Cassell and Co. 1916, p 21.

2 Comrie, John D. History of Scottish Medicine, Vol. 2. London, UK: Wellcome Historical Medical Museum, p 737. https://archive.org/stream/b20457273M002#page/737/mode/1up

Chapter 2: A Healer in Action

CHARLES TUPPER RETURNED from Scotland to Nova Scotia as a young man with ambition and prospects of a fine career. He must have been one of Nova Scotia's most eligible bachelors. Soon after returning to Nova Scotia in 1843, Tupper broke off an engagement he had made when only 17 years old. His second fiancée was the daughter of a prominent Halifax merchant, but their engagement was brief and broken. The woman he did marry was Miss Frances Morse, granddaughter of the founding family of Amherst. Through her, he made connections that would serve him well in politics.

A Rural Medical Practice

To earn his living, Tupper opened a medical practise. When his brother Nathan graduated from medical school in Philadelphia, he returned to Amherst, and they formed a partnership in 1845. The brothers worked not only as doctors, but as apothecaries. They diagnosed illness, compounded medicines, and treated injuries for people not only in Amherst but in the surrounding area.

During his apprenticeships, Tupper had learned the importance of getting to his patients. In rural areas, there were no ambulances to transport ill or injured people, so instead the doctor travelled to the patients at their homes and farms. When close to home on good roads, which were something like a gravel road or a dirt road in the country today, he drove a horse and wagon. "In his sleigh, carriage or saddle, he went from place to place, sometimes in deep and drifted snow," wrote his biographer Saunders, "and at other times in mud more difficult than the worst snow drifts."[1]

He kept more than one riding horse for going over rougher roads, which in poor weather could be as bad as a muddy hiking trail. If Tupper had a patient in the morning, and another in the afternoon, he could ride a horse to exhaustion before a day was over. There was so much travelling to be done that Tupper had to stable horses at several barns throughout Cumberland County.

He would borrow horses as well. It was not uncommon for a farmer to go to his stable and find Tupper's fine horse there, resting. Meanwhile the farmer's horse had been borrowed by Tupper who was making house calls.

People were quick to welcome the doctor into their homes if he paused there to change horses. One evening, he rode into the yard of a country home to leave the horse he was riding, and asked for a cup of tea. By the time the water boiled, he had fallen asleep in a chair. No one was able to wake him for hours. When Tupper woke, they got his wagon and horse ready, and he drove thirty kilometres home after dark. It had been a long day in which he'd treated three patients. He later claimed to have travelled 160 kilometres by wagon, and another 80 on horseback, or some 170 miles in all, during that day. That particular tale seems to have grown considerably in the telling, as there aren't enough hours in a day to go that far at the speed of a horse.

19th Century Doctors

While there was no health insurance or hospital in Nova Scotia at the time, people looked after public health in other ways. The duties of a nurse were done by the patient's family or sometimes a church worker, as Tupper's mother used to do during the scarlatina epidemic. Since there was no government health ministry charging taxes to pay health care workers, when Tupper cared for a patient he charged fees for his services and medicines.

Not all of Tupper's patients could afford to pay him in cash for treating their injuries or making medicines for their illnesses. Some would make payments by giving the Tuppers a chicken or farm produce such as eggs and vegetables. One patient even paid his medical bill by shoeing Tupper's horse. As well, any community lucky enough to have the services of a doctor did what they could so the doctor's home had all the coal and firewood it needed and hay for the horses, at little cost. "We may not have had any money to pay our doctor," said one small-town man who was raised in a log cabin, "but we made sure he never had to haul hay for his horse or cut firewood and risk hurting his hands."[2]

Even with many rural patients paying in barter, Tupper's income for his first year of practise was 400 pounds sterling – or about $14,000 in a time when $84 could rent a house for a year. Medicine was a profitable line of work! He had high expenses too, owning good horses and a fine carriage, but there was money he could invest. Loaning money for mortgages brought him a good return on investment.

Though the medical care he offered was not of a standard comparable to 21st century hospitals, there was no faulting his dedication and willingness to serve his patients. In years to come, Tupper was to brag that he never refused a sick call. It was said of him that if Tupper gave up on you, you might as well turn your face to the wall and die. When the wife of a political rival was ailing, Tupper stayed up all night, giving her doses of champagne every half-hour. The treatment probably benefited his reputation with her husband more than the woman's recovery, but at least it relaxed the woman and eased her pain.

A doctor in the 19th century often had much less training than Tupper. His own brother Nathan had a more brief education in Philadelphia before joining him in their medical practice. But even a year's apprenticeship with books to study was more than most people ever had. Doctors were very respected persons, and people tended to trust their opinions in general, not only on medical matters. For the rest of his life, Tupper benefited from that respect – and made sure no one forgot he was a doctor.

Learning Politics

During the early years of his medical career, Tupper was not yet a politician. He was not ignorant of politics, though, living in a colony that had a representative government since 1758. And he made good impressions on prominent politician Alexander Stewart, a lawyer who served on Nova Scotia's Legislative Council from 1838, as the member representing Cumberland County. Stewart served on the Executive Council from 1840 until 1846, when he was appointed to be a judge.

It was at a public debate in 1843 between Stewart and Joseph Howe, a Liberal, that Tupper first saw politics in action. Though Tupper had to leave right after the debate to go to a patient, the next day he ran into Stewart and introduced himself. The politician could see the young doctor's enthusiasm as he described his impressions of the debate. Here was a young man with a future!

A fierce opponent of responsible government for Nova Scotia, Stewart was one of those who believed that if Nova Scotia became independent of Britain, the colony would soon be swallowed up by the United States of America. That fear of American imperialism was not lost on Tupper, though he supported responsible government. The impression that Tupper made was not lost on Stewart, who thought well enough of the young doctor to introduce him to his niece, Frances Amelia Morse, the daughter of his sister.

Happily Married

It's easy to understand why Frances Morse and Charles Tupper were soon married. They were of a good age to get married, for one thing: when they married on October 8, 1846 she was twenty years old and he was twenty-five with his medical practice to support them. He was a good-sized man about 5 feet 9 or 10 inches tall (about 177cm), which would make him stand out in a time when many people were small from malnutrition. He was also confident and good-looking, which would only add to his appeal.

Frances was a fine-looking woman herself, and intelligent. She came from a family very well regarded in Amherst. Her father had inherited wealth, but he had lost most of his money lending to people who built homes but were unable to pay him back; he worked as the chief clerk of Nova Scotia's Supreme Court. Frances had many suitors, but it was Charles that she chose to marry. Though Frances did not have as big a dowry as might be hoped, her family had not lost connections to relatives and friends. These connections were a big help to the Tuppers as their income improved and needed to be invested.

When they were married, the young couple moved into half of a large, elegant house that her father had recently built. It was handy to have her parents living in the other half of the house, as Frances was soon expecting their first child. Tupper was able to be away treating his patients, but know that Frances had her mother close at hand. When their daughter was born in July 1847, they named her Emma. Their second child was born two years later, in April 1849. They named her Elizabeth Stewart, and called her Lillie. Frances was an Anglican, not a Baptist like her husband, but he agreed their children would be raised in her faith.

Hard Times

Their fine house did not last more than six weeks after Lillie's birth. Both little girls and Frances were lucky to escape a fire that destroyed all their possessions. That day Tupper set out to see a patient, but for some reason he turned back to look in the direction of home. He saw smoke rising, and flames. Racing back towards home immediately, he was horrified to find their home was on fire. As soon as he knew his wife and children were safe, he ran to the stable, but the fire had spread too quickly to be stopped. Neighbours held Tupper back from going into the burning stable to save a favourite horse. There was nothing that could be done but watch their home go up in smoke.

The fire was the beginning of the darkest time for the Tuppers. They lost little Lillie on November 30, 1850, to dysentery. Adults could sometimes survive the severe diarrhea and vomiting caused by this disease, while a child is more vulnerable. Though Tupper had saved more lives than he could count, he was not able to save his own daughter. It was a sad event, but not uncommon in those days before modern antibiotics and intravenous replacement of fluids. In the 1800s, a high mortality rate among children under two years old was an accepted fact of life, as it still is in some Third World countries.

Tupper's own mother died the next summer, which was another grief, though the loss of aging parents is to be expected. Perhaps the strain contributed to Tupper falling ill with typhus, a disease that can be carried by lice and fleas. But their lives took a turn for the better in October 1851, when Frances gave birth to their first son, James Orrin Stewart Tupper.

An Important Name

Cumberland County got its name when the Planters came to Nova Scotia. The grandfather of Frances Tupper (neé Morse) was one of the founders of the town of Amherst in this large county on a peninsula connecting most of modern-day Nova Scotia to the mainland area that came to be called the colony of New Brunswick. Living there were many Scots and people of Scottish descent, as could be expected when the Acadia colony was re-named Nova Scotia by the British. Scots would remember the Jacobean rebellion in 1743, when Scots lost to the English at the battle of Culloden. The English commander there was Lord Cumberland, and his name was given to this county when it was founded. While the farms were being developed and the town improved, that name would be recognized by every Scot as a deliberate choice, to emphasize that the English were in command here, not the Scots nor the French nor the Mi'kmaq. It's worth noting that in his later years, Tupper was known to many as the Old Warhorse of Cumberland County. Every time his riding's name was spoken or read from a newspaper, Scots would be aware of that name.

A Call to Serve

As hard as Tupper worked, all the health problems of a maritime county could not be solved by a doctor rushing around over rough roads. He formed some strong opinions, and decided he could express better ideas than some of the speakers at public events. Taking the stand at a little rural meeting in March 1852, Tupper spoke in support of Conservative candidate T.A. DeWolfe. He made a good impression on the crowd, some of whom were members of the Conservative party. Invited to make DeWolfe's nomination speech the next day at a gathering of 3,000 people, Tupper accepted.

On the way to the meeting, he was so nervous that he had to stop to be sick. But after throwing up, he headed for the stage and was ready to take his turn. Joseph Howe was late arriving, so the organizers invited Tupper to begin without him. At Howe's last-minute arrival, there began a dreadful argument as to whether the nominators or the candidates should speak first. The dispute lasted an hour, and Tupper wasn't shy about taking part. Finally, Howe made the mistake of letting him go first. Tupper launched a verbal attack against the Liberal government, impressing the crowd. Howe was appalled at being upstaged.

These two men had met shortly before the event, in a home where young George Johnson (later Dr Johnson and Statistician for the Dominion of Canada) lived with his parents. Both Howe and Tupper happened to be visiting when the head of the household announced that it was now nine o'clock in the evening, and time for family prayers. The household knelt, and their visitors too, as the host devoutly prayed for "the blessing of heaven upon the two strangers within the gate, and ask that they might be animated with a strong sense of duty in their public life."[3]

That strong sense of duty did drive both Tupper and Howe, and their lasting rivalry began at that nomination event. This wasn't the only time Tupper spoke his mind in public – on other occasions, Tupper spoke at public events and promoted his opinions about ways the current party in power was not meeting the needs of the colony.

In nearby Saint John, New Brunswick, a dreadful epidemic of cholera killed 1500 people during just eight weeks in 1854. This loss of life happened in spite of the quarantine station set up at Saint John since 1785. At the station, immigrants who showed any signs of illness were disinfected – at least on the outside – by being showered in kerosene, and then hot water, while their clothes were steam-cleaned. This treatment was helpful for reducing diseases carried by lice and fleas, such as typhus, but it did nothing about disease germs inside the bodies of people. Quarantines and cleanliness were not enough, and Tupper came to realise that public health in the colony needed to be managed by government in more effective ways.

Local members of the Conservative party knew that if they were to serve the colony in government, this well-known doctor was their best hope of taking the seat in Cumberland County from the Liberal incumbent. It was hard to convince Tupper to run for office; he worried that his medical practise would be ruined because his patients would be neglected while he was campaigning. As well, on August 3, 1855 his wife had just given birth to their second son, whom they named Charles Hibbert. Finally, Tupper agreed to run for office in the election of 1855, on the condition that when the party no longer needed him, he would quit.

1 Saunders, Edward Manning. *The Life and Letters of the Rt Hon Sir Charles Tupper, vol 1.* 1916. New York, NY: Cassell, 1916.

2 Johanson, Bertie Johan. In conversation with the author, discussing his youth in a small, isolated town in the Coal Branch of Alberta. 1980.

3 Hammond, M.O. Canadian Confederation and its Leaders. New York, NY: G.H. Doran, May, 1917. Electric Canadian website. Retrieved June 10, 2015. http://www.electriccanadian.com/ makers/confederation/chapter15.htm

Chapter 3: A Vision for the Future

IN THE COLONY OF NOVA Scotia's legislative assembly, Tupper was the member representing Cumberland County from 1855 until Confederation in 1867. During his twelve years as first an MLA and later as the premier, he was part of the cabinets that enacted powerful new laws for the colony. He introduced the jury law for trials, and the Equity Judge act. The education act founded a system of free public schools and assessment. Important infrastructure was built, with the Windsor and Annapolis Railway Act which built a second railway line, and the construction of a quarantine station and a hospital. The representation bill and the executive and legislative disabilities act confirmed government responsibilities.

In Nova Scotia, the leader of the Conservative Party was James William Johnston, a friend of the Tupper family and a fellow Baptist. It was Johnston who encouraged Tupper to take an active role in politics by running for office.

"He entered public life at the age of thirty-four in his native province of Nova Scotia," Sir Robert Borden was later to write for the introduction to Tupper's memoirs. "And during the twelve years which ensued before Confederation, his public record gave abundant evidence of the magnificent courage, the fine optimism and the breadth of vision which invariably characterised him in the wider arena in which he was destined to play so distinguished a part."[1]

A Unique Colony

Nova Scotia was in a unique position in the British Empire as of 1848: it had a responsible government. Through ten years of advocacy, Liberal politician Joseph Howe succeeded in convincing Britain to allow the colony to elect not only its legislative assembly, as it had done since 1758, but its executive council as well. It was the first British colony to govern itself, with a British governor as the Crown's representative to sign into law the bills passed in the legislature.

Howe's home riding was Cumberland County, where Tupper lived as well. When an election was called in 1855, Tupper ran for a seat in the Nova Scotia Assembly, against Joseph Howe who was the incumbent and premier. When speaking in public, Howe took every chance he could to make fun of the yokel country doctor, but it wasn't enough to win him the vote. Though Tupper won his seat, that 1855 election was lost by the Conservatives, with the Liberals winning a majority of seats. Howe was not pleased to be out of the Assembly. When teased about having lost his seat to a political newcomer, Howe retorted that in his opinion, it would soon be true that he had lost it instead to the new leader of the Conservative party.

At the first meeting of the Conservative caucus, January 30, 1856, Tupper spoke up for a new strategy of promoting common interests with the Roman Catholic minority among the citizens. Though Johnston spoke often in the House of Assembly during that session, it was Tupper who challenged the government with acerbic speeches that were so partisan, Premier Howe called him "the wicked wasp of Cumberland."

In years to come, Howe was frequently an opponent of Tupper's on many issues that arose. When members of the Liberal party who were Roman Catholic found increasing strain in their relations with Howe, Tupper encouraged them to cross the House and join the Conservatives. By the end of February 1857, even having a new leader wasn't enough to keep a Liberal majority in the House. The Conservatives took office on February 24.

Toe the Party Line

Joseph Howe and the Liberals strongly believed in government construction of railways. While James William Johnston led the Conservatives, their party supported instead the idea of private construction of railways with government subsidies. Toeing the party line, Tupper shared Johnston's views in public discussions. Johnston offered to resign as leader in Tupper's favour, but as a newcomer to the assembly Tupper preferred to learn the work rather than claim the title of leader. He knew he had much to learn. Johnston became premier then, and before long Tupper was appointed his provincial secretary. Within a few months he was doing many duties for the Cabinet, and it was clear Johnston was preparing him to lead the party.

The first speech Tupper made in the assembly as provincial secretary laid out ambitious plans for railroad construction. One of the needs Tupper perceived for Nova Scotia was a reliable transportation route among the British colonies in North America. His argument was that the mines of Nova Scotia held inexhaustible minerals and coal that could support manufactured goods marketed throughout the east coast of North America. An intercolonial railway from Halifax to Québec City would move lumber and coal from the Maritimes and manufactured goods and grain from Canada East and Canada West. The expense of such a railway was more than any one corporation wished to spend, and Nova Scotia's government could not bear the cost alone, even for the portion within its own border.

In June 1857, Tupper began discussions with Canada and New Brunswick, proposing an intercolonial railway. These discussions were not immediately successful. For the Canadians he spoke with, a far more important issue was expanding their union of colonies, but Tupper didn't have a mandate to discuss that topic. As for New Brunswick's legislature, they didn't want the expense of a railway any more than Nova Scotia did.

In an attempt to encourage the British government to invest in an intercolonial railway, Tupper travelled to London in 1858, bearing letters signed by representatives from Nova Scotia, Canada and New Brunswick.[2] The British prime minister then was the Earl of Darby; he and his Cabinet were occupied with their own interests, and those of India. At that time, the British secretary of state for the colonies was Baron Edward Bulwer-Lytton, who took more interest than the Cabinet did in the British colonies in North America. Lytton had sponsored the act creating the colony of British Columbia in 1858, but "he wasn't exactly the finest secretary of state the British Empire ever produced," noted writer Bernie Fandrich. "One historian of that time remarked that not all secretaries of state were incompetent; only Lord Bulwer-Lytton deserved that reputation."[3] Lytton did manage to present Tupper's petition, but it was unsuccessful.

Meanwhile, Tupper worked to increase development of mines. As he advised, Premier Johnston ended a monopoly the General Mining Association held on Nova Scotia minerals. An emerging theme was to become a dominant one throughout Tupper's career: that religious and ethnic differences among citizens should be downplayed as people concentrated instead on developing natural resources for industry and trade.

When Tupper succeeded Johnston as premier in 1864 with a large majority of seats in the legislature, he had no plan for the government to build a railway from Truro to Pictou County. But the assembly member for Pictou County, James McDonald, found many opportunities to insist on a railway to Nova Scotia's second largest urban centre. When McDonald became financial secretary in 1864, he pressed the matter and won approval from the cabinet. When the cabinet's decision was announced in the legislature, Tupper supported government construction of the railway with as much vigor as if the policy were his own idea. It was a typical move for Tupper, to support decisions that had been made by his party while in office, even decisions he had advised against at first. He didn't show any shame for changing his mind.

Living in the Capital

As provincial secretary and later premier, Tupper had no time to practise medicine in Amherst. He handed the practice over to his brother Nathan. Tupper moved his family to a home in Halifax, the capital city of Nova Scotia. Of course, it was his wife Frances' duty to manage their household, and she did so while raising their children and directing their few servants. Wherever the Tuppers lived in their sixty-five years together, Frances managed their home capably from its modest beginnings in Amherst to the fine houses of their later years. They travelled together when possible, a sign that they were an unusually close and loving couple.

In 1858, Frances gave birth to another daughter, Sophy Almon. There were advantages for a woman married to a physician: instead of being worn out with pregnancies every year, Frances was able to space her children's births from two to four years apart. The Tupperss's youngest son was born in the summer of 1862, and they named him William Johnston Tupper after the premier.

Though little Sophy died in 1863, the eldest daughter Emma kept her in memory. When Emma grew up to become a mother herself, she would name her first daughter Sophy, and later her younger daughter Lillie, in memory of her little sisters who died of childhood illnesses.

With all these children, Tupper might have been seen as a family man. But based on stories told about Tupper, he had a reputation as something of a ladies' man instead. There were rumours that horrified his wife, about his relationships with many other women. This reputation might or might not be a fair assessment, as it was a claim made by his political rivals. He liked women, and flirted gallantly, but he was a dedicated husband to Frances. In years to come, most of the rumours ended; but a century after his death, a resident of the Amherst area confirmed "there are local stories about Tupper's exploits, especially his propensity to 'get around' when travelling."[4]

While living in Halifax, the Tuppers acquired a pew at St Paul's, an Anglican church there – he and Frances made regular, planned donations, and a pew was set aside for their family's use during services. When on the campaign trail he frequently chose to attend Baptist meetings, where he would quietly make substantial offerings in the collection plate. These donations were expected from prosperous families, as churches were expected to provide for the welfare of people in need in their communities.

Active in Medicine

When the Conservatives were defeated in 1859, Tupper had time to establish a medical practise in Halifax, which brought him a handsome income. The city appointed him chief medical officer. Helping establish the Provincial and City Hospital, the first hospital in the colony, Tupper served there on the surgical staff. He also chaired the committee which established a medical school, in an effort to reduce the numbers of poorly-trained healers and outright quacks who called themselves physicians. As one of the best-trained doctors in the colony, Tupper worked to improve the profession. By 1863, there was a Medical Society of Nova Scotia, and they elected him to be their president.

For years to come, Tupper carefully maintained his professional image as a doctor. Under his desk in the Legislature, he kept his medical bag.

Administering Education

In 1862, an Act of Parliament in Britain re-opened Dalhousie College, which had been closed for twenty years. Charles Tupper was named governor of Dalhousie in its new standing as a secular college rather than a religious one. While there were excellent facilities for higher education in Nova Scotia, there was no system of public schools. Out of a population of 300,000 in Nova Scotia over the age of twenty, there were 81,479 people who could not read. There were at that time 83,959 children between the ages of 5 and 15, but only 31,000 were attending school in 1863.

Working in Nova Scotia's legislature, Tupper was able to support the foundation of a public school system, and had the courage to carry it out despite public impatience with the taxes necessary to fund it. In 1864, he proposed the Free School Bill, so that schools would be free from having to charge each student a fee. This bill was founded on the principle that every citizen should enjoy the same benefits and participate in the same liberties. The bill provided equitable means for the division and collection of taxes and would build schools in remote areas of Nova Scotia. The free school act was passed.

When Tupper became premier in 1864, the government of Nova Scotia established a system of public schools supported by compulsory taxation. These schools were non-denominational, with minimal religious instruction. Thomas Connolly, Archbishop of Halifax, put pressure on Tupper to create and fund a separate school system for Catholics. Tupper was firm in his refusal. The compromise he made allowed the one public school system to establish some school buildings for Catholic teachers and students. As well, he guaranteed there would be Roman Catholic involvement in the direction of the school system, by including Catholics as well as Protestants on local school commissions and the provincial Council of Public Instruction.

Sometimes Tupper preferred to deal directly with Connolly's assistant, Michael Hannan, who was less emotional and public with his emotions and endorsements. Baptist and Anglican pastors were not shy about approaching Tupper, either. Since his own youth, Tupper had noticed that religious controversy was not unknown in Nova Scotia. Under his political influence, the dissent between Protestants and Catholics was diminished in Nova Scotia, at least on the issue of public schools. Twenty years later, the North West Rebellion and the execution of Louis Riel would renew hard feelings between Catholics and Protestants throughout all Confederation.

Tupper in 1865

Extravagant Utterances

"In the period of transition from Provinces to a Dominion, leaders and people were all prophets, the minority of evil, but the great majority of good," wrote Tupper's biographer Saunders. "Many extravagant things were uttered by both classes of political seers. While no one was more assured of a grand future than Dr. Tupper, no man among all the politicians of that day equalled him in heroic, tireless efforts to bring about his predictions – no one was his equal in going hither and thither over the Dominion, and everywhere rising above local prejudices, making the audiences, which were held spellbound by his assured declarations, feel that the Hon. Charles Tupper belonged to no province but was a citizen of Canada who felt the loyal pride of this new citizenship. This spirit was contagious. The increase of Canadian sentiment was intelligent and rapid."[5]

Long-Winded Speeches

In the 1800s, it was common for public events to include speeches from officials of all kinds. These speeches commemorated special events, visits from dignitaries, and offered opportunities for grandstanding and repetition of the speaker's opinions and goals. Speeches lasting an hour or more were common, and enthusiastic speakers could end up orating for two or more hours. It was a time before the invention of radio and television broadcasts. People gathered for these events and seemed to welcome the opportunity to fall under the spell of an effective public speaker such as Tupper, whose personality was larger than life.

"He lived and thrived in an age of strong words," wrote M.O. Hammond. "Nova Scotians were wearying of ornate orators, and his energy and bluster were as invigorating as a northwest wind. His deadly earnestness carried weight, his fighting manner roused friends and cowed his more meek opponents."[6] He brought listeners under his spell. In public debates, it was hard for any speaker whose turn came after Tupper to maintain the same effect on the assembly. After Tupper gave a speech, nobody following sounded as warm or as confident as he did. He was a hard act to follow.

In debates, it didn't help his opponents if they spoke first, for Tupper didn't ignore them as he waited his turn to speak. "For exposed joints in the harness of an opponent, Sir Charles Tupper had the eye of an eagle," wrote his biographer Saunders.[7] Tupper was always alert during debates for admissions by the other speakers, which would give him a new supply of ammunition for his arguments. He was particularly fond of *ad hominem* arguments attacking his opponent personally as a way to discredit his opponent's ideas, which he seemed to compose while speaking. Of course, he also had plenty of time to compose while listening to an opponent's speech. These personal attacks were effective in changing opinions among his listeners.

He would bully his way through to win a debate or win over a crowd or finish presenting a statement in the Legislature. He fought with words and wouldn't back down from his opinions, always confident that he was fighting for what was right.

Colonial Union Goals

Tupper had come to the conclusion by 1860 that it would be best if all the colonies of British North America formed a union. Lecturing at the Mechanics' Institute in Saint John that year, he went so far as to advise that this union should include even the settlements at Red River and Saskatchewan. Like many people, he believed that without this union, many if not all the colonies would be taken over before long by the Americans. By 1864, he proposed a Maritime Union colonies, as it seemed an immediate union of all the colonies would not be possible. A meeting was scheduled in Charlottetown, PEI, for delegates visiting from New Brunswick, Nova Scotia, and Newfoundland to discuss Maritime Union. Representatives of the Province of Canada requested to attend this meeting to present their own proposal for a larger union of colonies.

The Charlottetown Conference became the first of three conferences leading to the confederation of Canada as a nation. Tupper led the Nova Scotia representatives at all three conferences: the Charlottetown Conference during the first week of September 1864, the Québec Conference a month later, and the London Conference of 1866. Before the London Conference, Tupper was a delegate to England on public business from Nova Scotia's government in 1865, and during that visit he did much to set up the conference.

There was an anti-Confederation movement active in Nova Scotia, organized by Joseph Howe; accordingly, Tupper organized the Confederation movement to counter Howe's efforts. He was successful, mostly because of timing. The Conservatives had won an election in 1864, and did not need to go to the polls again for years. With some fast talking and promises to get a better deal for Nova Scotia within Confederation, Tupper had his mandate to lead Nova Scotia into Confederation.

1 "Introduction" by Rt Hon Sir Robert Borden, KCMG, in The Life and Letters of the Rt Hon Sir Charles Tupper, vol 1 by Edward Manning Saunders. New York, NY: Cassell, 1916, p v.

2 "Message (item 4)." Appendix to the Journals of the Legislative Assembly of Canada, Volume 17, Issue 1. Toronto, ON: Rollo Campbell for the Legislature, 1859.

3 Fandrich, Bernie. British Columbia's Majestic Thompson River. Lytton, BC: Nicomen Publishing, 2013, p 147.

4 Bragg, Jaimie. In Facebook conversation with the author, discussing his youth in Amherst, NS. 2016.

5 Saunders, Edward Manning. The Life and Letters of the Rt Hon Sir Charles Tupper, vol 1. 1916. New York, NY: Cassell, 1916, p 231.

6 Hammond, M.O. Canadian Confederation and its Leaders. New York, NY: G.H. Doran, May, 1917. Electric Canadian website. Retrieved June 10, 2015. http://www.electriccanadian.com/makers/confederation/chapter15.htm

7 Saunders, ibid.

Chapter 4: Confederation

CANADA, UNDER THAT name, began as a united province of the colonies previously known as Ontario and Québec, now Upper and Lower Canada. Macdonald was elected in 1844 to the legislature of the united Province of Canada. By 1857, he was premier of this colonial government. No party proved capable of governing for long in this colony's unstable political system. In 1864 Macdonald agreed to a proposal from George Brown, his political rival, that the parties unite in a Great Coalition to seek confederation among the British colonies in North America. Their subsequent conferences and discussions led to the British North America Act, creating Canada as a new nation on July 1st, 1867.

Tupper as an Agent for Confederation

For Tupper, the separate British colonies in North America were so unconnected politically that the citizens did not have their interests well represented internationally. "What is a British-American, but a man regarded as a mere dependent upon an empire which, however great and glorious, does not recognize him as entitled to any voice in her Senate, or possessing any interests worthy of imperial regard," he said in a landmark speech in 1860. "British America, stretching from the Atlantic to the Pacific, would in a few years exhibit to the world a great and powerful organization."[1] Ideally, the emerging colonies in the western part of the continent would be developed and form a union with the rest.

By 1864, Tupper chanced his focus to concentrate on what seemed a more practical goal for the present: a union of the Maritime colonies as a preliminary to a national federation. When a conference was set to take place in Charlottetown, PEI, it was attended not only by delegates from Nova Scotia,

New Brunswick, and Prince Edward Island, but representatives of Newfoundland as well as Upper and Lower Canada. The discussion shifted from a Maritime union to a larger confederation. Tupper was one of those who proposed significant independence for provinces within a centralized union.

Back at home in Nova Scotia it took much political work for Tupper to overcome opposition from Joseph Howe, but eventually in 1866, Tupper succeeded in getting the Legislative Assembly of Nova Scotia to vote in favour of union. In exchange for Howe's support for Confederation, he and Tupper worked together for better terms for Nova Scotia's interests in Parliament. Though Tupper was expected to be given a post in the first Cabinet, he stood aside so other representatives from Nova Scotia would be appointed to that role.

The Charlottetown Conference

A Colonial Addressing Britain's Parliament

It's hard to know for sure exactly what sort of impression Tupper made in Britain. While his biographer Saunders wrote of Tupper as an august and honoured man, not everyone he met was as deeply impressed by Tupper, particularly during the early years of his political career. To represent first the colony of Nova Scotia and later the new country of Canada, Tupper had to mingle with people whose education, travel, and sophistication could make him feel aware of his more modest experience. Others, such as the Fishmongers Company, were astute men of business in fields where labour was key. Those differences would never have stopped him; Tupper was brash and bold, and confident of his own abilities. He threw himself into projects with enthusiasm. But in Britain, he was far from home and wouldn't have fit in easily anywhere.

There was the matter of his accent, at the very least. In Britain, even today a person's accent identifies his or her birthplace through distinct regional differences. As well, a person of noble birth or education can be recognized in a sentence or two. In the 19th century, an unexpected or inappropriate accent could discredit a public speaker and distract listeners from his or her message. As the descendant of colonists Tupper did not have an upper-class accent, nor would he speak like the men educated at the colleges in Oxford and Cambridge (smoother than the radio and television announcers on the BBC network today). Instead, he probably sounded something like people in Nova Scotia do today, with a flat accent influenced by the Scottish colonists and by his time in Edinburgh.

Tupper was an opinionated person who came to Britain to represent the interests of a colony. And represent them he did, with rather more enthusiasm than many of his listeners must have had, both in and out of Parliament. He was a long-winded public speaker who didn't get to the point of his statements quickly. Based on a reference to him in a novel serialized in the Dublin University Magazine, when Tupper addressed the House it may have been rather boring for listeners. In the novel, a character Guy sends his lady Vivian a note asking to dine with her after leaving Parliament that evening – a poetic note as she has requested:

> *O subject for a boyish shout!*
> *O theme for Tennyson or Tupper!*
> *Vivian, the House is counted out –*
> *Guy Luttrel will have time for supper.*
> *Thanks to this opportune eclipse,*
> *A dozen bores have found oblivion.*
> *Ice your champagne, but not your lips,*
> *And smile a welcome, darling Vivian!* [2]

Humour is shown here, by using two-syllable and three-syllable rhymes. This poem makes Tupper sound like a writer of epics that ought to hold our interest (but often don't). At any rate, it's interesting to see Tupper as a figure in the media of his time. This reference was the 1865 equivalent of being skewered on comedy television by CBC's Rick Mercer and Mary Walsh, or Stephen Colbert.

If Tupper did not inspire admiration in all the people he met in Britain, some of those people did inspire him to imitate them, if not admire them. Photographs of Tupper show that before his first visit to England, he was clean-shaven. By the time of his next visit, he had grown an impressive set of mutton chop side whiskers. This style of long, bushy sideburns had become popular in Western Europe. It began as a military fashion, and perhaps was inspired by hussar regiments. In strong contrast to the 18th century, when almost every European man living west of Poland was clean-shaven, during the 19th century military men began wearing beards and mutton chops, and the fashion spread.

Without an Intercolonial Railway to expedite travel between the Maritimes and the river valley of the St Lawrence, the province of Lower Canada could seem overwhelmingly distant from Halifax or Saint John.

Tupper knew better than to risk holding an election on the issue of Confederation, as he might lose. Since his government had been elected in 1863, he didn't have to call an election until 1867.

April 1866 brought news from New Brunswick's legislature. "On Caldwell's authority the Governor had turned out of office an anti-Confederation government and brought in a pro-Confederation one," noted Craig Brown in his Illustrated History of Canada. Tupper sprang into action. "He got a Confederation resolution through both houses of the Nova Scotia legislature that same month."[3] Though Prince Edward Island and Newfoundland were not confirmed to support Confederation, Nova Scotia and New Brunswick were enough to form a union with Upper and Lower Canada.

If it seems from a 21st century perspective that the Fathers of Confederation were rushing into this union with surprisingly little time for discussion and negotiation, there was a reason. American influence was growing in British North America. In Nova Scotia, some tempers were still hot over raids from nearly a hundred years earlier during the American Revolution, but other colonists had strong ties to their roots in American states. Would it be sensible for Nova Scotia to become an American state? Some thought so. Thousands of Nova Scotians fought in the American Civil War, most of them on the side of the northern Union. Britain remained neutral during that war, and so trade continued between Nova Scotia and both the Union and the southern Confederacy.

With the end of the American Civil War, there was a strong movement in the United States to acquire British North America. In July 1866, a Bill was read in the US House of Representatives to admit British colonies, and the western territories that had formerly been controlled by the Hudson's Bay Company.[4] There was no time to wait.

The Fathers of Confederation at the Québec Conference

Tupper was instrumental in getting the colony of Nova Scotia to agree to join the new confederation of Canada. Archbishop Connolly gave what help he could to the movement for Confederation. In an effort to support the creation of a funded separate school system for Catholics in Nova Scotia, he attended the London conference of 1866-67. He found sympathy for his request from the colonial secretary Lord Carnarvon, and from other delegates, but not enough from the Nova Scotia delegates. Tupper was firmly opposed to separate schools, and would not grant the archbishop's demand. Later in April 1867, Connolly tried to get Tupper to introduce legislation in Nova Scotia's House of Assembly to fund a separate Catholic school system, but Tupper remained firm.

Knighthood

With the terms of union completed, the British North America Act was signed into law by Queen Victoria in April 1867. The country of Canada was considered to exist as of July 1, 1867. Macdonald was appointed the first prime minster for Canada, and asked to form a Council or Cabinet from a coalition of Conservative and Liberal members of Parliament.

For their services to the new Dominion of Canada, Queen Victoria dubbed both Macdonald and Tupper as knights, companions in the Order of the Bath. This honour is given mostly to military officers, and occasionally to civil servants for service of particular merit. Tupper returned home as Sir Charles Tupper, C.B.

At home, not everyone was impressed with his knighthood. Particularly dismissive were Liberals and anti-Confederation activists who called him "the Boodle Knight", saying his knighthood was a bribe. That year he was called "the most despicable politician within the bounds of British North America" in the pages of the *Halifax Morning Chronicle*. Newspapers of the day didn't even pretend to have a neutral stand on politics.

The Nova Scotia Difficulty

He was sent right back to England in March, 1968, as a delegate from the Dominion Government with respect to the Nova Scotia difficulty. That's the name given to an unfortunate event that nearly broke up Confederation less than three months after it began. In Nova Scotia, the Conservatives lost a vote of confidence in the Legislature, and so an election was held on September 18, 1867. Joseph Howe led the Anti-Confederation party to a majority in that province. In the provincial legislature, the Anti-Confederation party won 36 out of 38 seats, and 18 of Nova Scotia's 19 federal seats. Howe seized the opportunity to send petitions to Britain requesting that Nova Scotia be allowed to leave Confederation. There were some thirty thousand signatures on the petitions, and Tupper had to contradict them in Britain's Parliament, insisting that elected officials had fairly represented their citizens.

"Dr Tupper is a man of whom I will say nothing that is disrespectful," stated the Right Honorable John Bright, considered the finest orator in his generation, when addressing the British Parliament. "He is a man, I should say, of rather a subtle intellect, and he has what is an admirable thing in a Prime Minister – a persuasive tongue, and, what is more, he appears to me to have an ambition which is not willing to be confined within the comparatively narrow limits of the Province of Nova Scotia, and, somehow or other, Dr Tupper managed to convert the minority of the year before into the majority of the year 1866, and succeeded in having this Resolution passed and these delegates appointed."[5]

The only Quaker in the British Parliament, in the recent past Bright had spoken out to present minority views on several important issues. He had advised against Britain fighting in the Crimean War, for example. Now, he took seriously Britain's receipt of petitions from 30,000 Nova Scotians to release their province from Confederation, and wondered aloud how Tupper and the Fathers of Confederation had succeeded in forming their Resolution for union and getting Britain to approve it. It took some fast talk from Tupper that is not recorded in Hansard, but somehow he persuaded Britain's prime minister and cabinet that the mandate for Confederation was solid, and alternatives to union would be disastrous. As well, after returning to Canada Tupper and Macdonald eventually convinced Howe to support Confederation by promising better terms for Nova Scotia.

Newfoundland and Confederation

The crown colony of Newfoundland and Labrador sent delegates to the conferences debating confederation. Representatives attended the Québec Conference in 1864, and to Tupper's delight they even signed the resolutions from that conference, which became the foundation of the British North America Act. Throughout the 1860s, confederation was debated actively in Newfoundland. Their 1869 "confederation election" saw that issue hotly argued among the candidates. The anti-confederates won by a landslide. Newfoundland became the only British North American colony to work seriously for independence within the British Empire.

In 1887 Tupper visited St John's, Newfoundland, to raise the matter with both government and opposition members of their legislative assembly. A coalition among factions could have carried a vote, but it came to nothing. Tupper reported back to Sir John A. Macdonald that former premier William Whiteway changed his mind about associating his party with confederation at that time. In 1895, Tupper was an interested party in official negotiations about the possibility of Newfoundland joining confederation, but those talks ended without resolution.

From 1929 to 1940, the Great Depression's world-wide economic effects hit Newfoundland particularly hard, contributing to a collapse of responsible government in 1934. During World War II, the relationship between Canada and Newfoundland was changing. By the end of the war, confederation was being promoted by Canadian and British government representatives. A 1948 referendum showed a bare majority of Newfoundlanders agreed. In 1949, Newfoundland and Labrador became the latest British colony to join the confederation of Canada – but not the last, if the little colony of Grand Turks and Caicos ever succeeds in its intermittent efforts to join Confederation.

Scots Names

In every British colony could be found a great many Scots and descendants of Scots. Before Confederation and afterwards for many years throughout Canada, the names of Scots were very common. Many of these Scots had come to Canada for work with the fur trade. Some names such as MacKenzie or McDonald occurred over and over, frequently with the same first names as well. Informally, a man in Nova Scotia might need to introduce himself as "Angus Fraser, Ian's Davy's Angus from Sydney," naming his father and grandfather as well. For Tupper at least, a less common name was a valued asset. During the 1860s and 1870s there was another Tupper active in Britain's Parliament, but no other Tupper in Canada's House of Commons. Canada's first prime minister is often spoken of in our history as Sir John A., after he was knighted, to distinguish him from the other men named John Macdonald who were active at that time in Canadian business and politics.

Ripple Effects of Tupper's Stand on Education

When Confederation took effect July 1, 1867, responsibility for education was placed in the jurisdiction of each province, not as a federal concern. Previously, schools had largely been independent of government because they were financially self-sufficient or supported by private funding. The law governing public schools in New Brunswick, the Common Schools Act, was based on the Tupper Law that was passed in Nova Scotia in 1864. Passed in 1871, the Common Schools Act was met with protests from Francophones and Catholics, who appealed to the federal government against Anglophone controls over schools. By 1875, it took an armed insurrection in Caraquet, quelled by the militia, to get a few concessions made to the rights of Francophones by the New Brunswick government.

As well, when the Manitoba Act became the basis for the creation of Manitoba as a province in Confederation, it specified a separate school system for Francophones in that province. By 1895, the issue of separate schools for French-speaking Catholics in Manitoba would be appealed to the federal government, and became the issue that would bring Tupper into office as prime minister.

But when Confederation was new, Tupper maintained a correspondence with Archbishop Connolly, on the subject of how best to support the new Confederation. Connolly wrote to both Tupper and Macdonald with his impressions of many people and how to enlist their support. As well, he sought favours for those who supported Confederation, no matter whether they were Catholic or Protestant.

For a backbencher without a seat in Macdonald's coalition Cabinet, Tupper was unexpectedly active speaking in the House. He seemed confident in his influence. "His natural pugnacity and initiative carried him along in the House," historian M.O. Hammond later wrote, "while Sir John Macdonald soon learned to lean heavily upon him, though he was not yet in the Cabinet."[6]

1 Buckner, Philip. "Tupper, Sir Charles." Dictionary of Canadian Biography, Vol 14. Toronto,ON/ Laval, QC: University of Toronto/Université Laval. Revised 2015. Retrieved December 2, 2015. http://www.biographi.ca/en/bio/tupper_charles_14E.html

2 Herbert, George. The Dublin University Magazine: a Literary and Political Journal, Vol. 65 # 388. Dublin, UK: W. Curry, jr & Co., April 1865, p379.

3 Brown, Craig, ed. Illustrated History of Canada, 25th anniversary edition. Montréal,QC: McGill-Queen's University Press, 2012, p322.

4 Bill HR 754, page 1. United States Congress, July 2, 1866. Washington, DC: Historical Collections for the U.S. National Digital Library http://memory.loc.gov/ll/llhb/039/4300/ 43090000.gif

5 Bright, John. "Anti-Confederation Petition from Nova Scotia." Hansard. London, UK: House of Commons, June 16 1868, v192 p1665.

6 Hammond, M.O. *Canadian Confederation and its Leaders.* New York, NY: G.H. Doran, May, 1917. *Electric Canadian* website. Retrieved June 10, 2015. http://www.electriccanadian.com/ makers/confederation/chapter15.htm

Chapter 5: Into the West

THOUGH HE WAS ONLY a backbencher in the House of Commons, without a seat in the cabinet, Tupper ended up helping to settle a controversy at Red River Settlement, a controversy considered by some Canadians to be a rebellion. He travelled from Ottawa to Fort Garry in what is now the province of Manitoba, successfully negotiating with Louis Riel. With that success, he was brought to the cabinet and became a representative for Canada in negotiations with America.

Hard Times in Red River

Hardly a year after Canada's formal beginning, the new government negotiated with Britain and the Hudson's Bay Company to bring Rupert's Land into Confederation as the Northwest Territories. Tupper was busy then, so Canada sent George-Étienne Cartier and William McDougall to Britain as its negotiators.

Somehow, no one thought to explain this imminent transfer of jurisdiction to First Nations people who had lived for thousands of years in small villages throughout the vast lands that drained into Hudson Bay. No notice was given either to the settlers living in Selkirk territory, Red River Settlement, or the parts of the territory known informally as Assiniboia and Saskatchewan. Without warning, an announcement was suddenly made in Red River that the Company was no longer responsible to Her Majesty Queen Victoria for the territory, and that Canada now would be, as of December 1, 1869. The news was not popular among either the French-speaking residents of the territory or those who spoke English. Their petition in 1857 to join the provinces of Upper and Lower Canada had been ignored.

This sudden annexation could hardly have come at a worse time. The summers of 1868 and 1869 brought hardship for the Red River Settlement, as their crops were destroyed by grasshoppers and drought. Hunger was inevitable. The Canadian government started a relief program, bringing food and supplies for men employed to construct the Dawson Road between the North West Angle and St Boniface. Among the men who took this relief work were mostly settlers, and very few Métis. In spite of back-breaking work for credit at a store in St Boniface rather than for cash, little progress was made on the road. Most Métis were justifiably suspicious of this program; unable to read or write, many depended on their priests and particularly Bishop Taché to translate government papers and advise them. Unfortunately, Taché was visiting Rome during the summer of 1869.

When Macdonald sent surveyors in August 1869 to set the meridian lines for the Settlement, there was no one to explain to Métis farmers why their long, narrow farms were being re-surveyed in a grid pattern. This surveying didn't look at all like preservation of existing farms before an expected influx of new setters to the territory; to Métis farmers it looked like their land was being appropriated for re-distribution to new settlers. When surveyors came to André Nault's farmland half a mile west of the Pembina Road, Nault and his neighbours went to his nephew Louis Riel for help. Riel had spent ten years in Québec, and had the education to be a teacher and a lawyer's assistant; as well, twenty years earlier Riel's father had mobilized the Métis to settle a freedom of trade matter with the Hudson's Bay Company. With permission from the local priest, Father Ritchot, Riel would meet with Métis who needed assistance at the presbytery, or church offices, in St Norbert. On October 11th, Riel was catapulted into a leadership role among the people of Red River Settlement. Their provisional government declared its loyalty to the Queen, and rejected annexation.

Rejecting the Lieutenant Governor

Meanwhile in Ottawa, William McDougall was appointed the new Lieutenant Governor for the North West Territory. He and his party made their way to Red River Settlement via American railways south of the Great Lakes. As assistant to McDougall, Donald Roderick Cameron had brought his young wife – Tupper's only daughter, Emma. Having been married that July in Halifax, the Camerons were newlyweds, but already well-travelled in their journey from Halifax to Ottawa and then to Red River. It was planned that Donald Cameron would command a mounted police force in the new territory; a veteran from service in India, he was a Captain in the Royal Artillery. Cameron had a fine gun and was a good shot, after adjusting his monocle. Among the Métis he was gaining a reputation as a mannered fool.[1]

The approach of the designated Lieutenant Governor was observed by Métis who reported back to Red River Settlement. "On October 20," noted historian D.N. Sprague, "Métis witnesses to McDougall's arrival at Saint Cloud [now a city in Minnesota] came home to report that they had seen several cases of the latest repeating rifles in the Canadians' baggage." The party was travelling with sixty carts of McDougall's luggage and furnishings, but a large portion of this luggage was firearms: 250 Peabody carbines and 100 Snider repeating rifle carbines new in cases of ten, as they were issued from Ottawa stores along with 10,000 rounds of ammunition. In addition there were many hundreds of blankets and coats, and an unconfirmed number of hundreds of common muzzle-loading rifles. These carts were Red River carts, a two-wheeled wagon locally made with a few simple tools. The carts were pulled by an ox or horse, and carried a load weighing about 225 kg (500 lb) or more, about the size of the payload of a modern pickup truck or an El Camino. The Camerons had brought only a single carriage of trunks.

At Pembina on the border between American territory and Rupert's Land, McDougall's party was halted, first by a dispatch from the provisional government which ordered them not to enter the Territory of the North West without special permission, then on November 2nd by a roadblock on the only good road from Pembina. A large barrier of fencepoles blocked all but a narrow path, and a band of Métis guarded their roadblock confidently. Their provisional government was refusing entry to McDougall. Guards confiscated the McDougall party's luggage in the name of the provisional government, and firmly refused to allow them to go any farther toward Fort Garry, where the Hudson's Bay Company had maintained offices. There was no other way to travel, until later in winter when the rivers would freeze. The lieutenant-governor's party was stalled. When the news reached Ottawa November 16 via telegraph from jeering American newspapers, it was humiliating for the new Canadian government.

A Man of Action

In the early winter of 1869, Tupper was the man the Canadian government sent to negotiate at Red River Settlement. Macdonald was able to apply himself only partially to the issue, as the "crushing burden of personal financial troubles and family sorrow had pushed him into nearly continual drunkenness in the autumn of 1869."[2] In a few days, Tupper and Macdonald scraped together a rough plan: to get McDougall out of the North West Territory, to delay paying England for the transfer of the Territory until the resistance was over, and in a few days to send to Red River Donald Smith (until then, the HBC's top man in Canada) and a pair of representatives from Québec.

Then Tupper set out to Red River himself at once, hoping to reduce the impact of McDougall's bungling. As well, he wanted to assure himself of his daughter's safety and to request the return of her goods that had been seized at the barrier on Pembina Trail. He was becoming the Conservatives' warhorse, not only for the party as he traveled throughout the eastern provinces during elections campaigning for other members of the party, but for the government in its negotiations with Canada's neighbours and new regions.

His journey to Red River became an odyssey. To reach Pembina in Dakota Territory was more than a simple ride on a railroad; Tupper had to transfer nine times to different railways as he travelled through American territory south of the Great Lakes. Then he rode in a wagon for ten days,[3] a rougher ride than he was used to from making his doctor's rounds in Nova Scotia. Practical as Red River carts were, the wheels turned with a piercing screech. The axles were not greased, as dust from the prairie would clog the grease and the cart would grind to a halt.

His passage was made somewhat easier when it became known that he was a doctor. "When knowledge of his profession became known, he was called many times by the Métis to attend their sick, which he did without hesitation," reported historian Nan Shipley.[4]

On the morning he crossed the border back into Canada, he was riding in a dog-carriole with a Métis driver only seventeen years old. He bought a horse for the driver. The sled he later described as "a large canvas shoe on a toboggan."[5] In his memoirs, he would later write that the temperature dropped to -30°F in a frozen fog that caused Tupper and his young driver to become lost. Tupper got out to lead the way, trying to follow the North Star through gaps in the fog. He claimed it wasn't until 10:30 pm by his watch that they found some tracks to follow to a Métis shack and the end of that long day's travel. The family of wheel-makers made their visitors welcome. They ate together sitting on the earthen floor of the humble home, and slept there until daylight.

In the Pembina area, Tupper arrived at the log cabin where his daughter Emma was keeping house for her husband and McDougall, her maid having fled. Startled by her father's sudden arrival, she blurted out, "But what are you doing here?"

What Did She Mean?

The appearance of Tupper on the scene, twenty-five hundred kilometres by rail and rough trail from Ottawa, was certainly a surprise for his daughter. But what did Emma mean by her question? Was she asking him why he was there at all, as if there were no worries? No. Her husband and McDougall had spent a month taking turns patrolling their temporary home in expectation of imminent attack, without proper rest or even changing their clothes. Emma was no fool. She'd been home alone there when an alarming visitor came in, a First Nations man wearing paint and feathers who spoke no English or French; sensibly, she cooked this stranger a substantial meal which he ate happily before leaving.

Perhaps she wondered why instead of a troop of armed soldiers, the prime minister had sent a man with no military service, almost fifty years old. Was she wondering what he thought he could do, or relieved that he was here for this crisis? Was she afraid of what he might do?

Tupper's appearance on the scene in mid-December revealed not only that he was a concerned father taking care of his daughter, but that he was acting for the federal government. He was able to de-escalate one element of the situation almost immediately by insisting the ineffective McDougall must return to

Ottawa. Because of Tupper's influence then and over the next two weeks, Canada's role in the matter of the Provisional Government of Red River became a negotiation into Confederation rather than an annexation.

Tupper in 1870

Tupper Signature

A Quiet Meeting

On New Year's Day 1870, the barricade was still in place on the Pembina Road, and the temperature rose to only -30F. The Métis guards waved Tupper through their barrier when he said he wished to speak with Father Ritchot.

In St Norbert, Tupper mistook the convent for the presbytery, but the sisters (including Riel's own sister) informed him the priest was in nearby Fort Garry, visiting Riel at his new headquarters in the former HBC base at the joining of the Red and Assiniboine rivers. The Mother Superior allowed Tupper to write a letter to Riel. When a sleigh arrived to deliver the letter, Tupper walked out to the light cutter and brazenly leapt on beside the driver. "Since you're going to Fort Garry I may as well deliver my message in person," he said.[6]

In Fort Garry, Tupper was escorted past an honour guard of 200 armed Metis volunteers to meet Louis Riel in his office, with Father Ritchot and Ambrose Levine attending. Their conversation would have been in English, for Tupper's sake; while he could read French and write it to some extent, he did not have Riel's bilingual education. At Tupper's request for the return of his daughter's property, Riel agreed that a Métis living in St Norbert would return these goods. Historian Shipley reports that there was no political discussion during this meeting, but others report that there was. Considering Tupper's history of debating his opinions with any opponent, and his role as a colonial representative in England, it is hard to believe he could meet Riel without discussing any political options for Red River and Canada.

The meeting was a success, from Tupper's point of view in particular. While talking with Father Ritchot with a nun as interpreter, Tupper succeeded in confirming that Riel's provisional government should send a delegation immediately to Ottawa, concerning their resolution to enter Confederation as a province rather than being managed as part of the North West Territory. Soon after, during a quiet social evening with Riel and several local people, Tupper kept the conversation light and off politics.

The delegation was sent from Red River as Tupper recommended. In fact, with hard travel over 2,000 kilometres in late winter and great good luck, the hardy delegates arrived before Macdonald could finish preparing a military response to the events in Red River. The provisional government of Red River negotiated its way into Confederation before summer as a brand-new province named Manitoba, with Louis Riel elected as one of its first representatives in Parliament. Undeterred by Manitoba's new provincial status, Macdonald's cabinet (now including Tupper) sent troops anyway. As the Dawson Road was hardly begun, Colonel Garnet Wolseley brought his troops by Lake of the Woods and the Winnipeg River, enduring seventy-eight portages before arriving months later to Fort Garry, which had been abandoned that morning.[7]

At a later date, Riel quietly entered the House of Commons and swore his oath as a Member of Parliament. Though three times he was elected as a representative for Manitoba, he was never able to take his seat while the House was in session, and so Riel and Tupper were never able to meet in Parliament. Due to the execution of a criminal in Red River, months after the meeting with Tupper and unconnected to it, Riel became regarded by some Ontario MLAs and MPs as a traitor to the crown. This rumour was whipped up in Ontario by John Schultz who had escaped from prison for leading some would-be vigilantes against Red River's Provisional Government. Remarkably, Riel's sister Sara remained in correspondence with Tupper for the rest of her short life, and on occasion he sent donations for the orphans in her care.

Tupper with grandchild November 1870

Results for Tupper

The results of Tupper's mad dash to Red River were important in a personal sense. The first result, and easiest to assess, was his relief at ensuring that Emma and Donald Cameron left the area with him in January, returning to Ontario. A few months later in April 1870, Emma and Donald Cameron announced the birth of their first daughter, Sophy, who was Tupper's first grandchild. That year, Donald Cameron translated into English Bishop Taché's book on the North West (*Sketches of the North West*), which perhaps helped him be seen by his father-in-law as more of a scribe than a mannered fool of an English gent.[8]

As well, Tupper had shown himself to be the government's man of action, and one not subject to Macdonald's long, alcoholic binges. With his family secure, Tupper was sent to Washington to deal with another concern for Canada: the inequality of trade with the United States of America.

In the House of Commons, Tupper spoke out on the advantages of a National Policy – the most important element of it was that high taxes and duties would be charged when manufactured goods were imported from other countries.

"Should we allow the best interests of the country to be sacrificed," he said, "or uphold a bold national policy which would promote the best interests of all classes and fill our treasury? . . . Whoever read the discussions of Congress would see that all we had to do was to assume a manly attitude on that great question in order to obtain free trade with the United States. But suppose they resented that retaliatory policy? The result would be hardly less satisfactory than a reciprocity treaty. It would increase the trade between the Provinces, stimulate intercourse between the different sections of our people, and promote the prosperity of the whole Dominion. Such a question should be fully considered, for it affected the most important interests of the country, and, properly dealt with, would diffuse wealth and prosperity throughout the Dominion."[9]

The speech was impressive enough that Macdonald not only brought Tupper into Cabinet, but made him President of that council. No longer a backbencher, Tupper was elevated to a position where international relations, the entry of a new province, and treaties with First Nations peoples in the North West Territory were all happening under his supervision. Among his first acts was to secure a Cabinet post for his old political rival Joseph Howe.

Tupper as president of the Canadian privy council in 1871

A New Province

The Manitoba Act created a brand-new province in Confederation, "but against all expectations, it did not allow the Métis to keep the benefits for which they had fought," wrote historian Luc Guay, speaking of the Métis' territorial, administrative, and commercial rights which had been recognized by the Hudson's Bay Company. "As a result, many moved west in order to preserve their privileges."[10] These Métis joined communities to the west of the North West Territory in an area called Saskatchewan.

Tupper and the Cabinet appointed men to sign treaties with First Nations peoples in parts of the North West Territory; in the opinion of the government, this act obtained their consent to Canada's sovereignty. The first three of these treaties were signed in 1871 and 1873, covering a wide area near Winnipeg. As author Wab Kinew points out, Treaty #3 was "one of the few where the

Indigenous people recorded the promises that were made to them – a document that lists more promises than the Queen's version of the treaty but makes no mention of land surrender."[11] These treaties and the men negotiating them were approved by Cabinet while Tupper was president, and later minister of Inland Revenue. He was well aware of the content of every treaty, and the unequal negotiation process.

Because Manitoba had been accepted into Confederation with provincial status, not as a territory, land speculators believed there would be other provinces formed in the west. In 1871, the colony of British Columbia was convinced to join Confederation with Macdonald's promise that within ten years, a railway would be built from the coast to the rest of Canada.

In Fort Garry, soon part of the city of Winnipeg, local historians still remember that for many years after the entry of Manitoba into Confederation, traveling stage coaches would pause at the Sale River. There passengers were able to observe brush and logs piled by the road, where a barrier had blocked the Pembina Trail for the winter of 1869-70.

1 "Memorable Manitobans: Donald Roderick Cameron (1834-1921)". The Manitoba Historical Society. Revised April 20, 2008. Retrieved July 20, 2016. http://www.mhs.mb.ca/docs/people/cameron_dr.shtml

2 Sprague, D.N. Canada and the Métis. Waterloo, ON: Wilfred Laurier University Press, 1988, p42.

3 Schlee, Gary. "Tupper's odyssey to Red River." Canadian Prime Ministers. Web. Posted December 26, 2009. Retrieved January 19, 2016. https://canadianprimeministers.wordpress.com/2009/12/26/tuppers-odyssey-to-red-river/

4 Shipley, Nan. Road to the Forks. Winnipeg, MB: Stovel-Advocate Press, 1969. http://manitobia.ca/resources/books/local_histories/034.pdf

5 Gottfred, A. "Dog Sleds in the Northwest." Northwest Journal ISSN 1206-4203 Updated 2002. Retrieved March 20, 2016. http://www.northwestjournal.ca/IV5.htm

6 Shipley, op. cit.

7 McNicholls, Paul. "The Red River Expedition of 1870 – Inside the British Army's Last Campaign Into North America." Millitary History Now, posted April 23, 2020. Retrieved November 21, 2020. https://militaryhistorynow.com/2020/04/23/the-red-river-expedition-of-1870-inside-the-british-armys-last-campaign-in-north-america/

8 *"Memorable Manitobans: Donald Roderick Cameron (1834-1921)" Manitoba Historical Society. Revised April 20, 2008. Retrieved August 18, 2016. http://www.mhs.mb.ca/docs/people/cameron_dr.shtml*

9 *Hammond, M.O. Canadian Confederation and its Leaders. New York, NY: G.H. Doran, May, 1917. Electric Canadian website. Retrieved June 10, 2015. http://www.electriccanadian.com/makers/confederation/chapter15.htm*

10 *Guay, Luc, director. "The Métis Rebellion." Peace and Conflict. Vancouver, BC: Historica Foundation of Canada. Retrieved June 23, 2016. http://www.histori.ca/peace/page.do?pageID=233*

11 *Kinew, Wab. The Reason You Walk. Toronto, ON: Penguin Books Canada, 2015, p44.*

Chapter 6: The Railway

THE 1870S WERE A TIME when elections were won or lost on the campaign trail, and newspaper articles were no substitute for speeches in person. Tupper did not accept funds from the party nor government funds for extra expenses campaigning, drawing only his salary as a member of parliament and president of the Privy Council or Cabinet.

On the other hand, Macdonald was frequently out of cash and on several occasions had to be given money by the Conservative party to settle his bills. During the 1872 election, a corporation of American businessmen led by Canadian Hugh Allen made donations to Macdonald's campaign, hoping their Canadian Pacific Railway would get the contracts for the railroad to British Columbia.

During his campaign travels, Macdonald sent a telegram to Hugh Allan, asking for "another ten thousand" for campaign funds and saying it would be the last. The press was already writing articles protesting how many cash donations had been made to the federal Conservatives by Hugh Allan and American businessmen wanting to profit from the proposed railroads. The Conservative coalition under Macdonald did win the 1872 election with a minority, but a year or so later when Macdonald's telegrams were leaked by an aide, the issue blew up into a scandal. The Huntington scandal, some called it, but Tupper referred to it as the Pacific Scandal, since the proposed railroads were to run all the way to the Pacific.

Cabinet shuffles moved Tupper to the post of Minister of Inland Revenue in 1872, and during 1873 he became Minister of Customs. Though he had not known of the shady campaign contributions, he was not absolutely free from controversy. During the federal election campaign of 1872, Archbishop Connolly in Halifax had written a letter to Tupper supporting policies of the Macdonald government, and giving Tupper permission to use the letter as a public endorsement. In Halifax the Morning Chronicle newspaper condemned Connolly for peddling his influence and Tupper for accepting it. No mention was made of money changing hands, though – in strong contrast to the Pacific Scandal. In spite of Tupper's valiant defense[1] of his prime minister and cabinet, the coalition government lost a vote of confidence. The first government of Canada had been defeated in the House of Commons.

Tupper in 1873

Advising the Governor-General

During the early years of Confederation, the role of the Governor-General carried a great deal of political influence, as well as the nominal responsibilities which remain. When the vote of confidence was lost, it was time for the Governor-General to take action. But what action, exactly, should he take? At first, Lord Dufferin (who was then Governor-General), asked Macdonald to resign, so that a new government could be made by a coalition based on the Liberals instead. It was Tupper who convinced him to reverse his decision. His own description of this meeting is as follows:

"I called upon Lord Dufferin, who said: 'I suppose, Doctor, Sir John has told you what I have said to him,' and was answered in the affirmative. Lord Dufferin said: 'Well, what do you think about it?' I said, 'I think your Lordship has made the mistake of your life. To-day you enjoy the confidence of all parties as the representative of the Queen. To-morrow you will be denounced as the head of a party by the Conservative press all over Canada for having intervened during a discussion in Parliament and thrown your weight against your Government. Nor will you be able to point to any precedent for such action under British parliamentary practice.'

"Lord Dufferin said: 'What would you advise?' I replied: 'That you should at once cable the position to the Colonial Office and ask advice.' That was done. Lord Dufferin sent for Sir John Macdonald at two o'clock that night, and withdrew his demand for the resignation of the Government."[2]

Instead of the resignation of Macdonald's government, an election was called, as recommended by Tupper. Calling an election became the virtually automatic result of a failed vote of confidence for most of the next century, with the exception of the Byng/King crisis of 1924. Perhaps Tupper gave his advice in the belief that the Conservative coalition had a good chance of winning the election, but the Liberals were to take a majority of seats in the election which took place in early 1873.

Active in Her Majesty's Loyal Opposition

After the defeat of the Conservatives by the Liberals in the election of 1873, Alexander Mackenzie became the second prime minister of Canada. The Conservatives were active as the opposition party in the house, but Tupper took time to return to practising medicine. Meanwhile, Sir John A. Macdonald returned to the law, living in a house on St George Street in Toronto that became known afterwards as the "Premier's House" where two Ontario premiers would later reside. In Toronto and Ottawa, Tupper worked as a member of the Opposition during the winters, and in summers he worked as a doctor in St Andrews, New Brunswick. He apparently earned more from his medical practise than he had as a cabinet minister.

During the time Mackenzie was in office, that prime minister considered Tupper to be his rival as much as Macdonald was. When the Liberals presented their budget in 1876, there was a surprise element. A tariff on trade was set rather lower than the Conservatives had expected. All their criticism had been prepared to advise the reduction of a tariff that was being set too high by the Liberals. Tupper rose to the occasion, and spoke about the tariff, suggesting that it could be raised. Afterwards, Mackenzie crossed the floor of the House to speak informally with Tupper, teasing him about his speech.

"I went over to banter him a little on his speech, which I jokingly alleged was a capital one considering that he had been loaded up on the other side," Mackenzie told Member of Parliament James Young that evening. "He regarded this as a good joke and frankly admitted to me that he had entered the House under the belief that the Government intended to raise the tariff, and fully prepared to take up the opposite line of attack!"[3]

Whatever the challenge, Tupper rose to the occasion. During his years in Opposition he was a merciless critic of the Liberals' finance minister Sir Richard Cartwright. With a widespread financial depression, the Liberals were not able to bring the country to prosperity, and so the Conservatives gradually gained public approval.

"The House of Commons was not a place for the timid or the delicate. Charles Tupper," as historian Craig Brown noted, was "good at marshalling strong arguments for weak causes, but the House of Commons was apt to take its own debates with several grains of salt. ...It was a rough place, made more so perhaps by the two parliamentary bars. During night sittings in the 1870s, half the MPs would be under the weather."[4] While Macdonald kept on his desk in the House a waterglass commonly filled with gin, Tupper kept his medical bag under his own desk.

Under the Influence

Mackenzie was scrupulously careful not to reap personal financial benefits while in office, more careful than expected or necessary. He couldn't fail to notice how Tupper's personal wealth had increased during his political career, even while in Opposition, and the increase wasn't all due to the work of his medical practise. Networking had brought opportunities for influence and profit. As well, in the past Tupper hadn't been shy about assigning work for federal money to people he knew; neither Tupper nor his party considered these patronage appointments to be inappropriate, provided that the work got done.

And work did get done. During the 1878 election, Tupper kept an exhausting schedule campaigning in his home riding and in other ridings where new candidates needed the support and rhetoric of a reliable public speaker. "Both parties saw and admitted that the returning courage of the Conservative party emanated from the ubiquitous Dr. Tupper," noted his biographer Saunders.

"It was greatly to his advantage that he was entirely free from the Huntington scandal. He knew nothing of it. Not a dollar of the large contributions to the election fund had gone to Nova Scotia. From the first this was seen and admitted by friends and opponents, and left to him the advantage of exerting himself, being in no way weakened by personal connection with the scandal," wrote Tupper's biographer Saunders, years later. "As time went on, to neutralize the force of the charges made by the Liberal party which had proved the undoing of the Government, he attacked them, not for political weakness and unwisdom alone, but also for political wrongdoing in the use of money in their own elections."[5] The court trials and other revelations supplied him with facts in this direction, and Tupper never needed more than a few facts to fuel his fiery speeches.

The country was beginning to show economic improvements just before Macdonald and the Conservatives won the 1878 election. In this election Tupper won the seat for Cumberland County, together with the cousin of his wife Frances, Charles Townshend, another Conservative. Tupper represented the county federally, in Ottawa, while Townshend was the provincial representative. The international economic depression was improved, so much that English banks were now able to invest funds in railroads.

"Honest Alexander Mackenzie brooded on the vagaries of fortune and the disconnection between honesty and progress," noted writer George Bowering. "He could no longer afford his nice house in Ottawa, and had to sell it to his enemy Tupper, of all people. The businessman pursed his lips while inking the deal."[6]

Family Ties

With the purchase of that house in Ottawa, there was a new Tupper home for Frances to furnish and manage. It became a home base for their children, who were now grown and leaving the nest. Even though there were still persistent rumours about Tupper's tendency to flirt with other women or sleep with them, by all accounts he and Frances were a devoted couple. At the age of 52, Frances was still considered "a very fine and handsome woman," and she was his dedicated companion, "re-establishing the family home wherever political necessity dictated and accompanying Tupper whenever possible on his travels."[7]

All three of the Tupper sons would become lawyers; since there were no law schools in Canada's Atlantic provinces at the time, the Tupper sons were trained by being articling students with law firms. Most lawyers of the time operated either an independent practise, or a simple partnership of two lawyers. One of these partnerships expanded to become one of the first modern law firms in Canada and "a nursery of giants, producing three chief justices of Nova Scotia and two prime ministers."[8] Wallace Graham and R.L. Weatherbe formed a partnership in 1872, and student Robert Borden articled with them from 1874 to 1878. That year, a new partner joined the firm, John Sparrow David Thompson, when Weatherbe was appointed to the Supreme Court of Nova Scotia. The timing of that appointment to Queen's Council coincided with Tupper's middle son, Charles Hibbert, becoming an articling student. This timing was perhaps a coincidence. But by 1881, Tupper's influence was more overt: the firm of Thompson and Graham took Charles Hibbert Tupper on as partner, and their firm was appointed as agent of the Department of Justice in Halifax. That same year, Graham was also appointed to Queen's Council, as the elder Tupper arranged these favours in acknowledgement of favour given.

By 1882, Thompson had become a judge, and Charles Hibbert had been elected to Parliament to his father's delight. Work as an MP took Charles Hibbert Tupper away from the firm's day-to-day business when the House of Commons was in session, but Robert Borden was a partner now, and another associate was hired to assist with the work of this successful firm. Borden was a bright young man only a year older than Charles Hibbert, and became well acquainted with the Tupper family. Even after Charles Hibbert withdrew from the firm in 1888, the connections remained strong between the Tuppers and Thompson and Borden. Both young men became active members of the Conservative party.

Return to Power

When his party returned to power in 1878, Tupper allowed his medical career to dwindle during the passing years. He is still commemorated by the Canadian Medical Association, a hundred and forty years later, through the Sir Charles Tupper Award for Political Action. This award honours doctors who have demonstrated leadership, commitment, and dedication in advancing the goals and policies of the CMA through grassroots advocacy.

By 1879, Charles Tupper had been a fixer for the Conservative party for over a dozen years, and one of the ablest. Tupper bulldozed his way to success, whether winning elections or securing loans for government projects. He served as minister of public works from 1878 to 1879, and was the obvious choice for Canada's first Minister of Railways & Canals. In his role as head of the new department, it was his job to push the Canadian Pacific Railway across the Prairies to the west coast.

It's not hard to determine what the British government thought of Tupper. In 1879 (while Tupper was visiting England in a failed attempt to persuade the British government to guarantee the sale of bonds for construction of a railway), Queen Victoria knighted Tupper for a second time. On this occasion, he was appointed a Knight Commander in the Order of Saint Michael and Saint George. This order is a British honour conferred by the monarch, and people are appointed to this order to honour their important services to Commonwealth or foreign nations. Macdonald was knighted again also, and the same offer was made to Alexander Mackenzie, who refused the honour. Tupper returned home as Sir Charles Tupper, KCMG, with 50,000 tons of steel rails bought at a bargain price.

It is hard to be sure exactly what Macdonald thought of Tupper by this time. Rather than regarding Tupper as his heir apparent, Macdonald disagreed with him over what role Tupper's friend Sandford Fleming would play in the engineering of the CPR. This rift did mend to some extent, but never mended completely.

Familiar with the cities and landscapes of the eastern part of the Dominion of Canada, Tupper had not yet seen the farthest western province. In 1881 he travelled to the province of British Columbia to support the interests of the Canadian Pacific Railway. The journey to British Columbia began in Montréal, and went by rail through the United States, from Chicago on the Union and Central Pacific Railway to San Francisco. From there, Tupper and his party went by steamer and rail up the coast to Seattle, and steamer to Victoria.

There were banquets held in his honour, followed by large public meetings on the burning question of the day: the construction of a railroad connecting the west coast with the rest of Canada. Was such a railroad necessary? And if so, who would be responsible for its construction – and who would reap considerable expected profits based on its location? The intent was that Canadians travelling within the Dominion would not need to detour on a round-about journey through the United States as Tupper and his group had just done. Tupper was able to promise his enthusiastic listeners that within ten years, there would be a complete and unbroken railroad stretching from Halifax all the way to Vancouver. For some reason, they believed him, in spite of being told by Macdonald the same thing back in 1871. In fact, the Canadian Pacific Railway would be considered completed on November 7, 1885, when the Last Spike was driven in at Craigellachie in Eagle Pass, British Columbia. The actual last spike for the rail line would be driven by Macdonald with a silver hammer on August 13, 1886, twenty-five miles north of Victoria BC.

Profile Photo of Tupper

By 1881, Tupper had been working for twenty years to support his vision of a united British North America. His hard labours were now bearing fruit, and this sense of accomplishment brought enthusiasm to the speeches he gave in British Columbia. At one point Tupper in a steamer visited Burrard Inlet, inspecting the site selected for the terminus of the Canadian Pacific Railway. The steamer anchored at Hastings Mills, the site of present-day Vancouver (near the corner of Hastings and Main) where coaches waited for the party, with a horse for Tupper to ride, some nine miles to New Westminster. The probable route for this ride was the traditional First Nations footpath that has become a paved road known today as Kingsway, or Highway 1A.

Tupper returned to Ottawa via San Francisco and Winnipeg. He wrote in his journal that a wave of public approval met him wherever he travelled in the west. The physical challenge of travelling had only improved his health, and he noted that he had gained weight and felt a returning strength. "At no time in his life was Sir Charles in better spirits, in finer fettle, with his health perfectly restored, physical vigour at its best, and the ring of victory in all the shoutings from the Maritime Provinces to British Columbia,"[9] wrote his biographer Saunders.

A Statesman in Action for the Railway

At age sixty, after twenty-five years in public service, Tupper's popular image was based on more than just a chorus of applause during political crises. At this time he had earned the confidence of the Canadian public. While he was Minister of Railway and Canals, considerable money was spent on widening the Welland Canal as well as deepening portions of the Saint Lawrence Seaway and improving other canals, in addition to promoting the building of local railway routes, all of which benefited shipping and industry. Both parties in the House of Commons, the Conservatives and the Liberals alike, regarded Tupper as a distinguished personality and accepted him as a statesman, though abrasive and not to everyone's liking. In his home province of Nova Scotia he had shepherded a period of expanding prosperity as the railways were built, he had founded a public education system, and supported Confederation against all opponents. He believed that the Canadian Pacific Railway and the National Policy were to be solid cornerstones for Canada, bringing future prosperity and maintaining a connection with Britain.

THE HON. SIR CHARLES TUPPER.

Tupper Drawing From the British Library

Railway construction was certainly profitable for the contractors in British Columbia. As Canada's first Minister of Railways and Canals, Tupper was operating confidently and independently. The federal government signed the contracts he arranged, without debating and ratifying them in Parliament.

"The government gave the Canadian Pacific Railway Company, a private company started by a group of executives, $25 million in cash and almost 25 million acres of land suitable for settlement. Property used for railway purposes was to remain free of taxation forever. Equipment imported for building the railway was admitted into Canada duty-free," noted Bernie Fandrich in his history of the Thompson River Valley where the CP line was built. "The government passed laws that provided a virtual monopoly to the CPR for 20 years. It also agreed to look after the cost of construction of 342 miles of the western rail line – Port Moody (Vancouver) to Craigellachie near Revelstoke, the most challenging and expensive section of the entire line – and then donate it to the CPR."[10]

For this railway's construction from Vancouver to Savona's Ferry, the contractor was Andrew Onderdonk, the American engineer and construction contractor who at age thirty-seven was the front person for a group of wealthy American financiers. Onderdonk became a personal friend to Tupper, who was impressed with the American's experience in labour relations and balancing a budget. It was Tupper's preference that the government should work with one contractor for all five contracts covering 215 miles of the CP rail line through some of the roughest terrain in the country. Four of these contracts, covering the distance from Yale on the Fraser River to Savona on the Thompson River, were signed prior to February 15, 1881, when the bill outlining the terms and conditions for the railway was signed into law. Over a year before the Governor-General (then Lord Lorne) signed royal assent to the bill, Onderdonk's workers (with Tupper's approval) had already begun blasting rock to make a railbed, where gravel would be pounded and wooden ties set to support steel rails.

The plans Onderdonk had to balance his budget for this project involved hiring Chinese railway workers, some of whom were hired in job lots distressingly similar to slave auctions. These workers were paid half or less the wage of white workers on the same sites. In addition, Chinese workers had to pay for simple food and minimal shelter though white workers did not pay for their slightly better food and tents. These Chinese workers were assigned the most dangerous working conditions, suffering appalling injuries and loss of life. No health care was given to them. The lasting rumour to this day in that region is "there was a Chink buried under every tie", using a racist term that remains ugly and hate language even when historic. Onderdonk's own testimony before a Royal Commission confirmed over 600 deaths, or more than four per mile of that section of rail.[11] Estimates of up to 2,000 deaths along that section of rail have been made. Other estimates calculate an average of a death per mile along the entire CP route.

These working conditions could not have escaped Tupper's attention as Minister of Railways. On Tupper's watch, these working conditions were allowed. Onderdonk's actions would have been criminal under modern labour laws, and would have been illegal under the 1872 Trade Unions Act passed by Macdonald, if only there were a trade union protecting those Chinese railway workers. "It has been estimated that Onderdonk's plan to import Chinese railway workers reduced his cost of building the railway by 25 percent, a savings of between 3 to 5 million dollars," stated historian Fandrich. "Onderdonk, the Canadian government, and the CPR benefited from their labour. Because of the Chinese labourers, the railway construction progressed, and British Columbia wasn't annexed by the United States."[12]

A Macdonald-Tupper Partnership

As time went on, Tupper and other men with powerful positions in the Canadian government saw their sons grow to manhood and positions of influence. Tupper's daughter Emma and her husband Donald Cameron spent some years in Ireland, where he was in command of a Field Battery. Tupper was proud when his eldest son, James Stewart Tupper, became a lawyer and practised law in Toronto after his second marriage to the daughter of Alexander Galt, one of the Fathers of Confederation. In August 1882, James Stewart Tupper moved to the city of Winnipeg with his family to practise law. He joined Hugh John Macdonald, the only son of the prime minister, in a legal practise that Hugh had set up two months earlier. Their partnership, Macdonald & Tupper, took offices near the main intersection in town, which in years to come would be known as Portage and Main.

Before many years went by, Tupper's youngest son, William Johnston Tupper, would join the firm. In years to come, the son of James Stewart Tupper and the son of William Johnston Tupper were also to practise law with the firm. It's no surprise that the law firm of Macdonald and Tupper was to represent John Schultz of Red River; that litigious man was in court several times before and during his time served as an elected Member of Parliament for Manitoba, an appointed Senator, and lieutenant-governor of Manitoba.

May 1883

Payoff or Posting?

In 1883 a British Columbia contractor close to Tupper was awarded a two-million-dollar job for railway construction, though rivals submitted lower bids. The opposition suspected a payoff, and made accusations in the House of Commons that Tupper was receiving kickbacks. Tupper faced a legal challenge and demands for a full inquiry. He promptly left his retirement home in Vancouver and sailed with his wife Frances for London, far from the cry of scandal, to take a diplomatic posting.

As of the first of June, he was appointed Canadian High Commissioner, while still retaining the role of Minister of Railways and Canals. Perhaps Cabinet was worried that the returning commissioner would step into that ministry; Alexander Galt had been recalled after some intemperate promotion of the idea of federating all of Britain's former colonies. At any rate, Tupper obeyed the letter of the law which specified that Parliament should be independent from Britain – he drew a salary as minister, but not as commissioner. He did accept a residence in London and an expense fund.

His pay wasn't the only issue though, as pointed out by a writer of that time. Conservative newspapers in Canada "declared that so long as he accepted no recompense for his English office he rendered his role unassailable; but it was pointed out by a writer in the Week that duty, not emolument, was really the vital consideration."[13] How could Tupper promote the railways as a servant of the Crown while acting for them as a Minister?

At any rate, Tupper was kept busy in England for the rest of the year. A telegram came to Tupper in London from Macdonald in December 1883, saying: "Pacific in trouble: you should be here." Next morning came the reply: "Sailing on Thursday."[14] He was needed to defend the railway in the House.

The North West Rebellion

It's not clear why the decision had been made to set the CP railway following the South Saskatchewan River, rather than the originally proposed route which would have followed the North Saskatchewan River. Tupper was Minister of Railways when that decision was made to choose a route closer to the 49th parallel and assert Canadian presence close to the American border. Unfortunately, the northern route would have served better some of the people who lived in Saskatchewan, whether settlers, Métis, or First Nations. Construction of the railway fostered some of the many resentments which led in 1884 to the second declaration of a provisional government for an independent territory within the North West Territory, with Louis Riel as the head of its governing committee – or the North West Rebellion, as it was considered by the Canadian government.

The Canadian Encyclopedia says of the circumstances leading up to the North West Rebellion: "It was the climax of the federal government's efforts to control the Aboriginal communities as well as the settler population of the West. Aboriginal persons who had thought themselves oppressed after the treaties of the 1870s became subjugated and administered people."[15] Tupper's memoirs say nothing at all about the North West Rebellion, a significant and curious omission, though he was a member of the cabinet which received Riel's petition of Métis grievances and demands, and authorised a three-person commission to review and settle Métis and Half-breed claims in Manitoba and the Northwest Territories. When word of a skirmish reached Ottawa on March 28 1885, cabinet mobilized the militia.

A section of CP Railway in Ontario between Callander and Port Arthur (today's Thunder Bay) was incomplete when it was pressed into service to carry troops to suppress the North West Rebellion in the spring of 1885. Among the soldiers brought to Saskatchewan was Tupper's youngest son, William Johnston Tupper, who at age 23 served as a private in the Halifax Battalion. William wrote to his mother on April 5, telling of his enlistment "so that people would not be able to say that 'young Tupper funked his duty and is a coward'."[16] With a "splendid pair of water-tight boots" given by his brother Charles Hibbert Tupper, William set out with his regiment on April 11. The train had no sleeping accommodations, but was cheered by crowds in every community. The Halifax battalion served by manning the lines of communication between Swift Current and Medicine Hat, rather than seeing action against the Métis or First Nations. It was boring to protect the major transportation routes of the South Saskatchewan River and CP railway, but after the Rebellion was suppressed, the Halifax volunteers returned home July 24 as heroes to public celebration where Louis Riel was burned in effigy.

It is not surprising for cynical modern readers to learn that Riel was tried for high treason and hanged on November 16, 1885. Several Métis leaders went to prison, as did First Nations leaders Big Bear and Poundmaker, while others were hanged at public executions. As a member of the cabinet, Tupper would have been part of many discussions concerning the botched trial of Riel and petitions for remitting the death sentences. Canada was bitterly divided between English and French on this issue.

What is surprising is that among all the many published statements of Tupper, it is hard to find any public statements on the Rebellion. He made only a single oblique mention of the execution of Riel in his memoirs. He wrote that in May 1888 he gave up the post of Finance Minister which he had taken on in March 1887, after he and Macdonald did not agree on several decisions that Tupper felt would promote the railways and development. He told Macdonald he would return to England, serving as the High Commissioner but a cabinet minister no longer. As Tupper recalled their conversation, Macdonald urged him to remain, saying that Sir George Stephen (banker and president of the CPR) wanted Tupper to be Macdonald's successor.

"But you have already made pledges to Sir Hector Langevin," Tupper replied. "When you were in difficulties over the execution of Louis Riel, you told Langevin that he would be your successor if he succeeded in retaining the support of the French-Canadian Conservatives."[17] This excerpt is typical of his memoirs: brief narratives in which Tupper is recognised as the better man than those around him, and events (even ones which shook Confederation to its roots) are secondary to his virtues.

Lasting Family Connection

There was a lasting family connection for Tupper with Canada's western provinces. Two of his sons maintained their legal practise in Winnipeg for the rest of their lives. During his retirement, Tupper was to visit them there many times. His oldest son's daughter Marie left Winnipeg as an adult to travel with her grandparents and settle with them in England after 1900. Tupper lived to see his youngest son William Johnston Tupper run as a Conservative in 1914, though he lost to the incumbent, lost again in 1915, and was elected in 1920 in the Winnipeg riding. William also was appointed to be Lieutenant-Governor of Manitoba from 1934 to 1940, during the challenging years of the Great Depression.

The middle son set up his home in British Columbia, first in Victoria, then in the Vancouver area, while still representing Pictou County, Nova Scotia in the House of Commons. He and his wife bought a little island and had rock work done there for their summer home.

1 Hammond, M.O. *Canadian Confederation and its Leaders*. New York, NY: G.H. Doran, May, 1917. *Electric Canadian* website. Retrieved June 10, 2015. http://www.electriccanadian.com/makers/confederation/chapter15.htm

2 ibid.

3 ibid.

4 Brown, Craig, ed. *Illustrated History of Canada*, 25th anniversary edition. Montréal,QC: McGill-Queen's University Press, 2012, p337.

5 Saunders, Edward Manning. *The Life and Letters of the Rt Hon Sir Charles Tupper, vol 1*. 1916. New York, NY: Cassell, 1916, p 231.

6 Bowering, George. *Egotists and Autocrats: the Prime Ministers of Canada*. Toronto, ON: Penguin Books, 1999, p78.

7 "Tupper, Sir Charles." *Dictionary of Canadian Biography*. Retrieved March 20, 2016. http://www.biographi.ca/en/bio/tupper_charles_14E.html

8 Girard, Phillip. "GRAHAM, Sir WALLACE NESBIT," in *Dictionary of Canadian Biography*, vol. 14, University of Toronto/Université Laval, 2003–, accessed October 16, 2016, http://www.biographi.ca/en/bio/graham_wallace_nesbit_14E.html.

9 Saunders, op.cit. p317.

10 Fandrich, Bernie. *British Columbia's Majestic Thompson River*. Lytton, BC: Nicomen House Publishing, 2013, p247.

11 "Chinese-Canadian life on the Railway." *Chinese-Canadian History, The Critical Thinking Corporation*. Retrieved September 12, 2016. https://tc2.ca/sourcedocs/uploads/history_docs/Chinese-Canadian%20History/Chinese-canadian-life-on-the-railway.pdf

12 Fandrich, p254.

13 Collins, Joseph Edmund. *Canada Under the Administration of Lord Lorne*. Toronto, ON: Rose Publishing, 1884, p296. https://archive.org/details/canadaunderadmin00colliala

14 Hammond, op.cit.

15 Beal, Bob, and Rob Macleod. "North-West Rebellion." *Canadian Encyclopedia*. Edited April 3, 2015. Retrieved March 20, 2016. http://www.thecanadianencyclopedia.ca/en/article/north-west-rebellion/

16 Stanley, George F. "New Brunswick and Nova Scotia and the North-West Rebellion." *The Developing West*, John E. Foster editor. Edmonton, AB: University of Alberta Press, 1983, p82.

17 Tupper, Charles. *Recollections of Sixty Years in Canada*. London, UK: Cassell and Company, 1914, p208. https://archive.org/stream/recollectionsofs00tuppuoft/recollectionsofs00tuppuoft_djvu.txt

Chapter 7: The Old Warhorse

SOME PEOPLE CALLED Tupper the Boodle Knight, saying he hadn't inherited a proper title but instead was given a knighthood as a bribe or boodle. The word boodle has the same roots as pirate "booty." Patronage was a common feature of politics in Great Britain and Canada at the time, bringing jobs to career politicians and useful members of the public. The rewards of patronage could continue, with salary increases, promotions, or special contracts to supply the ministry of defence and other ministries. Some people were scandalised by patronage favours, as is more common now. Other people considered a moderate amount of these favours to be rewards for hard work well done.

When Mackenzie Bowell was Minister of Customs, he received a request from Tupper. A former chief justice of Nova Scotia, Sir William Young, asked Tupper if two iron summer-houses being made for Halifax's Point Pleasant Park could be brought from Glasgow without paying duty. Tupper passed his letter on to Bowell, asking "What can you do for Sir William?" Perhaps Tupper thought it sensible to request this favour, as Sir William wasn't buying the summer-houses for his own property. Perhaps he thought that he and his friends were entitled to such benefits.

Tupper's reputation was untainted by the Pacific Scandal from the 1872 election, as it could be proved that his campaign funds had accepted not a penny of donations from the railway investors. But by 1884, there were other allegations that he had accepted kickbacks from the executives of Canadian Pacific Railway

At that time, Tupper had recently retired from Ottawa to live in Vancouver with Frances in a fine home. When the allegations were going to have to be answered, Tupper was suddenly not there to answer them, and Canada had a new High Commissioner to serve her interests in London. It was hard for

Canadian journalists or members of Canada's House of Commons to pin him down about just how much his income and personal wealth had improved recently, and the source of that wealth.

Tupper while minister of railways and canals, September 1881

Commissions

When Tupper became Minister of Railways and Canals, he needed a private secretary. Clarence Chipman stepped into this role at the beginning of 1882. They made a good team, and continued working together after May 1884, when Tupper was officially appointed to be the second Canadian High Commissioner in London. There, Chipman was his secretary and accountant. Together they were responsible for Canada's contribution to the universal exposition held in Antwerp the following year – well, Chipman did most of the organizing. As well, Tupper ensured Canada's participation in the Colonial and Indian Exhibition in London in 1885, which made a lot of work for Chipman as the exhibition's accountant.

As Canada's high commissioner, Tupper worked in London to promote improvements in services for Canada. Because of his influence, a steamship service between Vancouver and China saw financial help from Britain in 1886. But then he received a cable from Macdonald, saying: "I cannot too strongly urge upon you the absolute necessity of your coming out at once, and do not like to contemplate the evil consequences of your failing to do so."[1] At Macdonald's request, Tupper returned to Canada to campaign for the 1886 election, resisting the return of Nova Scotia secessionism that was led by William Fielding.

The Conservatives won that election, and Tupper was brought back to Cabinet as the Minister of Finance in 1887. Then he was able to ensure that iron and steel were added to the goods protected by tariffs. He wanted to help Canadian industries grow, and he was in a position of influence to support that growth. Negotiations over the Atlantic fisheries took up months of Tupper's time in 1887-88, including travelling to Washington DC, with Chipman as his assistant. The experience led to a new job for Chipman on July 1, 1888, as chief clerk in the Department of Marine and Fisheries and private secretary to the minister, who was Tupper's son Charles Hibbert Tupper.

This wasn't the only family connection Tupper had in the Fisheries Commission; his son-in-law Donald Cameron was secretary to the Canadian Commission on Fisheries in Washington in 1887-88. It seems that Tupper was putting his position of influence to good use for the benefit of his family, something that his political rivals were quick to observe. But to Tupper, it didn't seem wrong to recommend his daughter's husband for this position, or for secretary of the Canadian delegation at the Paris Conference on Submarine Cables in 1883 – not wrong, at least, as long as the work got done. If someone had to do this work and earn government money doing so, he thought, why not choose one of his own people?

Spending Government Money

Unfortunately, Tupper seems to have defined "his own people" rather narrowly: his family and colleagues first of all, the active citizens of Nova Scotia second, and then citizens of Canada at its Confederation. He championed Canada's interests even over those of Britain and its former empire. Somehow, though, his sense of responsibilities and considerations did not extend in the same way to First Nations citizens as Canada took jurisdiction over Rupert's Land.

Under treaties signed with First Nations on the Prairies while Tupper was president of the Privy Council, the federal government had promised to help First Nations bands with their transition to farming in the style of Canadian and European settlers. Yet, as early as 1887, the amounts allotted to buy seeds and grain for this purpose were reduced sharply by Macdonald's government. Of course, Tupper knew what was being done – he was the Finance Minister at that time.

Did Tupper believe his government did right? It seems so. As well, he appeared to be entirely comfortable with spending half of the monies allotted to supporting First Nations on salaries for the government's "Indian Agents" and for agricultural instructors.[2]

Recorded in Hansard from the session in 1887 are statements by Sir Richard Cartwright, who had been Minister of Finance in Mackenzie's government a decade earlier, and was hounded then by Tupper from his Opposition seat. Cartwright took pleasure in putting similar pressure on Tupper. "As respects the decrease in the item, seeds and grain $15,674, I have no objection to the honorable gentleman trying to practise a much needed economy, but I doubt very much, in some of these cases, whether the actual results will correspond. The reduction in this case is enormous, being from $20,000 to $4,000."

Tupper replied calmly, "It is a gratifying decrease." In those days, members addressing the House responded to one another's statements in a more conversational fashion than the formal style of addressing the Speaker without interruption.

"We have seen these decreases over and again put down on paper in the Indian estimates, and then had $300,000 or $400,000 taken out by Governor-General's warrants and other means of the same description to make them good," Cartwright retorted. "I doubt from what we know of the extent to which cultivation has progressed on these Indian reserves whether the Government will be able to supply the Indians with the requisite seed."

"It is quite true there was great discrepancy between the amount taken out and the amount required, and that the Governor-General's warrant had to be resorted to, and I draw the attention of the officers of the Indian Department and of my right honourable friend to it," said Tupper smoothly. "I am assured these estimates have been made up with the most careful attention to that point, and it is believed they will not require to be supplemented."[3]

The transcript goes on to show the topic of discussion changing to cover contracts for supplies and transportation, and the definition of an "Indian" as opposed to a "half-breed" (terms which are now considered rude and racist), and how the expenses for supporting First Nations had been reduced in spite of increased salaries for the increased numbers of agents. Reading Hansard records from this time is far more frustrating than watching Question Period on CBC Television in the 21st Century. It was quite common in the 1880s for Tupper or other skilled speakers to address the House at length or to appear to answer questions without in fact saying anything which could be summed up as short, pertinent statements. Any reporting in newspapers or correspondence about what was actually said or done amounts to commentary and interpretation.

Medical Career Successes

After his formal education as a medical doctor in Edinburgh, Tupper maintained an active medical practise for many years. His focus on health care did not end when he entered politics. On the contrary, he campaigned for both Confederation and for the creation of the Canadian Medical Association at the same time, and saw both come into being in 1867. Though he was never anyone's best candidate for prime minister in the first years of Confederation, he was the founding president of the CMA for its formative years.

As High Commissioner to the United Kingdom from 1884 to 1887 and again from 1888 to 1896, public health was among his highest concerns. When it came to his attention that port inspectors in Liverpool had rejected three shiploads of Canadian cattle, Tupper went to investigate. Inspectors said the cattle were infected with anthrax. This was dreadful news. Not only would the entire shipment of cattle be condemned, but future shipments from Canada would be banned. Tupper knew only too well from his farming background just how much the emerging beef industry in Canada depended on having a market in England to sell cattle.

Luckily for all concerned, Tupper was not merely a bureaucrat and a diplomat, he was a medical practitioner with experience treating farm animals as well as humans. He rolled up his sleeves and dissected a sampling of the cattle from each shipload. He was able to prove that none of the shipments were diseased with anthrax. The beef industry was able to go on shipping cattle to Britain.

Crossing the Atlantic in the hold of a sailing ship was never pleasant for cattle. They could often be underfed or have no fresh air and exercise. It takes a trained person familiar with the signs of disease to know the difference between animals that have an infectious illness and animals that have been confined without proper care. In 1893 while Tupper was in England, he cabled Canada's Department of Agriculture to pressure them to inspect thoroughly animals being sent to Scotland or England. He also advised the Canadian government to request that two veterinary surgeons be sent from Britain to inspect cattle in different parts of Canada.[4] Inspection standards have improved since Tupper's day, in part because of his example, and ports maintain proper inspections and testing by certified persons.

Great Danger of Anthrax

Hundreds of thousands of animals and people died of anthrax infections each year until the 20th century. Tupper was familiar with the signs and symptoms of anthrax in both humans and domestic animals. When cattle or sheep are ill with anthrax it's not a simple matter. The bacteria forms spores which survive in soil for decades and remain infectious, reducing the value of land. Herbivores catch anthrax by eating spores on tough or prickly plants. Carnivores can catch anthrax by contact with infected meat, and even the wool or skin of sick animals carries spores. Animals sick with anthax are killed and burned at high temperature in an effort to kill the spores.

The first vaccine was developed in 1881 by Louis Pasteur. Anthrax is still common in countries without effective public health and veterinary programs. Mortality rates were as high as 85% before antibiotics, and now range from 25% to 40%. Survivors often have disfiguring scars. Anthrax has been used in bioweapons programs by governments of the United Kingdom, United States, Japan, Russia and Iraq.

Tupper as Canadian High Commissioner to the United Kingdom in his court dress, dated "about 1883" though 1885 or 6 is more likely

Accepting Honours

In 1886 Tupper was visiting London to represent Canada. He spoke privately in favour of Home Rule for Ireland, much as the provinces of Canada had distinct powers. He was given an honorary degree of LL.D. by the University of Cambridge, and the Freedom of the Fishmongers' Company on the same day. He even wrote to the Dean of the university regretting that he had to decline the honour of attending at Cambridge, because that would make it unable for him to arrive in London in time to dine with the Fishmongers' Company. The dean persuaded the company to postpone their dinner a few hours so that Tupper could attend the Convocation and catch a train to London for the dinner afterwards.[5]

Satisfaction

When Tupper gave up his position as Minister of Finance, he returned to his position as High Commissioner, this time drawing an appropriate salary as a diplomat. Resuming his duties in London, he became known as an outspoken advocate of imperial federation with the United Kingdom. Sir John A. Macdonald was not pleased with Tupper's views, but Tupper's political standing allowed him immunity from censure. Sometimes it was very convenient that an ocean separated them.

In 1888, in a moment that would have swelled any father's heart with pride, Tupper saw his son Charles Hibbert Tupper not only re-elected to the House of Commons, but made a member of Macdonald's cabinet as Minister of Mines and Fisheries. At 33 years old, C.H. Tupper had become the youngest cabinet minister to date, and would remain the youngest for over a hundred years. C.H. Tupper had little time to maintain his legal practise in Halifax, and his partners, John Sparrow David Thompson and Wallace Graham, had many duties. So with goodwill, their friend Robert Borden became senior partner in their law firm.

It was during this year that Tupper arranged an appointment for his daughter Emma's husband. Donald Cameron became the commandant at Royal Military College in Kingston, Ontario. Whenever Tupper came through Kingston, on his way between Ottawa and England or while campaigning for the Tories, he would visit with them there. It must have been satisfying for Tupper that all his sons and son-in-law were now well-established, as his oldest and youngest sons were active in their legal practise with Hugh Macdonald in Winnipeg.

This year also saw Tupper rewarded again by Queen Victoria, who made him a baron on September 12, 1888. The Baronetcy of Armdale in Halifax was created for him as a reward for his efforts on the Atlantic fisheries negotiations. Though among British peers a baron is not of much distinction, this title is rare in Canada. There are only nineteen Canadian baronetcies.

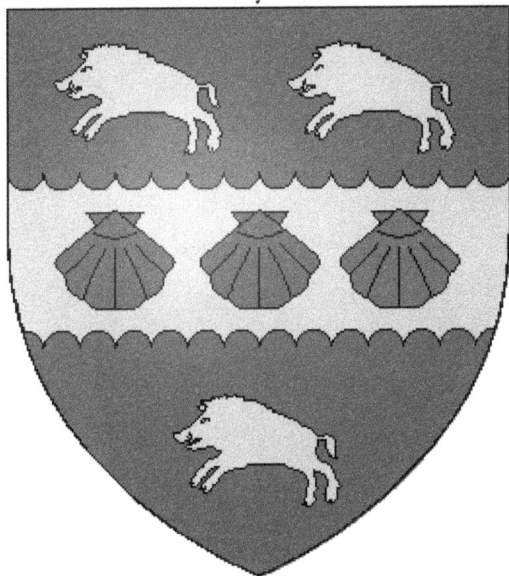

Coat of Arms

Power in Transition

At the age of seventy, Tupper was no longer a young man by anyone's standards. Photos show that he was growing a little stout, with a roundness of belly that fashion then called a "corporation" – which was considered a sign of wealth and health. Some of his grandchildren were adults, and his friends and colleagues were dying of old age. But he was in no mood to retire from his active life in England. His work earned him great respect among many government officials there. Living in London suited him well, as did travelling around Europe. He had no interest in returning to Parliament at that time.

He did return to Canada, however, when Macdonald sent for him to campaign during an election. "Sir John's last Macedonian cry was in January, 1891," wrote historian Hammond, "when he cabled: "Your presence during election contest in Maritime Provinces essential to encourage our friends. Please come. Answer." The war horse promptly responded, and in a few days "walked down the gangplank at New York with his usual springy step."[6]

While still High Commissioner, Tupper returned to Canada in 1891 to campaign against the policy being proposed by Liberals that Canada should have reciprocity with the United States of America. His opponents, both Conservative and Liberal, criticized him severely for taking sides in this matter. This issue was part of what made the job of prime minister so hard on Macdonald, whose health was suffering as it had before. This time, both Tupper and Macdonald could tell he could not hope to recover his strength. Though the election was won on March 5, when Tupper returned to his duties in England it was with the knowledge that Macdonald's health was failing. Now that Langevin was tainted with scandal in Québec and Ottawa, who would be Macdonald's successor?

Tupper with his son Sir Charles Hibbert Tupper and grandson, March 1891

While travelling in Europe that spring, Tupper received word from his son that Macdonald was dying. "I told you that nothing could induce me to accept the position in case the Premiership became vacant," Tupper wrote in reply, reminding his son of his last meeting with his prime minister and friend. "I told you that Sir John looked up wearily from his papers, and said to me: 'I wish to God you were in my place,' and that I answered: 'Thank God I am not.' He afterwards, well knowing my determination, said he thought Thompson, as matters now stood, was the only available man."[7]

When Macdonald died in office on June 6 of 1891, the party wanted continuity. Tupper remained as High Commissioner and John Thompson was the party's choice for leader. But Thompson stepped aside to let John Abbott lead Cabinet from his Senate seat. In the House of Commons, Thompson took the active role for a year, while Abbott led cabinet meetings. When Abbott was ready to retire, Thompson became prime minister, and Tupper continued spending most of his time in England.

Among the duties Tupper completed as Canada's High Commissioner was the successful negotiating of a commercial treaty between Canada and France in 1893. As a self-governing dominion rather than a British colony, the new country of Canada was learning to tread carefully in international politics. Somehow, as an agent for Canada, Tupper was expected to represent his home country's best interests while simultaneously keeping in mind the international obligations of Britain, which had a free-trade bias.

There were some nations to which Britain had granted "most-favoured nation" status as trade partners; under those treaties, "Britain was obliged to grant several countries as favourable a market in her colonies as was enjoyed by any foreign power," noted historian R.A. Shields. "Thus, if Canada granted tariff preference to France, a host of other nations could demand the same privilege." Should Canada, as a self-governing state, withdraw from this British sphere of influence or continue the association? Tupper's negotiations led to the Franco-Canadian Treaty. A hundred and twenty years later, this treaty continues to have lasting effects on Canada's international relations.[8] If Tupper had acted as carefully and equitably in treaty matters with the First Nations as he did with France in 1893, the history of Canada would have been very different.

1893 was also the year Sir Charles Tupper was proud to see his son Charles Hibbert Tupper distinguishing himself as a member of the Behring Sea Commission. The younger Tupper was representing the British government, which represented Canada's interests in that arbitration. Queen Victoria gave him a knighthood for this service, making the Hon. Charles H. Tupper now Sir Charles Hibbert Tupper, K.C.M.G.

Prime Minister Sir John Thompson passed away suddenly in December 1894 during an official visit to England. The logical choice for an experienced man to be prime minister was Tupper. Or it would have been, if Thompson and Tupper got along well. There were reasons Tupper had spent several years as High Commissioner, and one of them was that it kept him out of Ottawa. His party associates found his manners rough and abrasive. Thompson had made no plans for Tupper to succeed him as leader. Unfortunately, he hadn't groomed anyone else for the role. The unexpected death of Thompson at age 49 left an unplanned vacancy in Cabinet.

It was the duty of the Governor-General to appoint the next prime minister. At that time, Governor-General Lord Aberdeen held office. He didn't approve of Tupper, and neither did Lady Aberdeen. Her complaints of Tupper's rough speech and abrupt manners had an impact on Lord Aberdeen. To her, Tupper seemed dishonest and always on the lookout for money. Rumours were circulating again about his conduct with women outside his marriage. Besides, he wasn't even a cabinet minister at that time, so why should he lead Cabinet? Instead, Lord Aberdeen supported selecting a prime minister from among the Cabinet members.

The most senior cabinet minister was Mackenzie Bowell, who was named to the position of prime minister by the Governor-General. Bowell was thus the second Canadian prime minister to hold the office while serving as a senator rather than in the House of Commons. (John Abbott was the first, and there have been no others.) The particular virtue of Bowell as a prime minister was that he was not Tupper: not loud and assertive to the point of aggression.

Tupper January 1896

Manitoba Schools Question

Bowell and his predecessors had been struggling to solve the Manitoba Schools Question. When Manitoba abolished public funding for denominational schools in 1890, both Catholic and Protestant schools were affected. The decision angered French-speaking residents of Manitoba, who thought the decision was contrary to the Manitoba Act of 1870, in which provisions were made for French schools run by Catholics. A decision by the Judicial Committee of the Privy Council held that Manitoba was able to abolish public funding for denominational schools; but in a second challenge, the Judicial Committee confirmed that the federal Parliament had the authority to force Manitoba to re-establish funding.

SIR CHARLES TUPPER ET LE PARLEMENT

Cartoon of Tupper from February 1896

The problem seemed impossible for Bowell – or anyone before him – to solve. The country was divided over this issue, the Conservative party was divided over how to handle the matter, and even the Cabinet could not agree. The Tories had legislation already drafted that would force Manitoba to restore its Catholic schools, and Bowell approved of the draft. But opposition within his Cabinet made him hesitate, and postpone having the bill read in the House. It didn't help that as a senator, Bowell was unable to take part in debates in the House of Commons.

The government had other business to complete as well, but could not get to work with the House of Commons at a standstill. Bowell's own cabinet decided that he was the problem; he was incompetent to resolve this issue or lead the party while doing so. Seven cabinet ministers, including Sir Charles Hibbert Tupper (the second son of Tupper), hatched a plan to force him to step down.

On January 4, 1896 all seven resigned their cabinet posts, and then blocked any attempt to appoint successors. Bowell was livid, and denounced them all as "a nest of traitors." There was nothing he could do but agree to resign. After ten days, Lord Aberdeen had to intervene on Bowell's behalf as Governor-General. The crisis was resolved as six of the ministers were reinstated in Cabinet, and in a surprise move, Tupper himself filled the place of the seventh. Recalled from his post as Canadian High Commissioner to the United Kingdom, Tupper took a seat in the Cabinet as secretary of state. Elected in a by-election in Cape Breton, Nova Scotia on February 4, Tupper led the party for the end of this parliamentary session. He did not take the title of prime minister until Bowell formally resigned in his favour when Parliament was dissolved at the end of April.

The solution introduced by Tupper and his colleagues was legislation intended to protect the educational rights of Manitoba's French-speaking minority. The bill was blocked in the Commons by not only Liberal members of the Opposition, but some Conservative members who were unwilling to approve any bills put forward by the gang who had taken Bowell out of power. After torturous debate for six weeks during which all bills were blocked, Parliament had to be dissolved.

THE OLD FLAG! THE OLD GUARD
AND
THE OLD PRINCIPLE!

SIR CHARLES TUPPER—"I stand by the principle of ample Protection to Canadian Manufacturing Industries, and the extension of Protection to Canada's greatest Industry, Agriculture, by obtaining for the Canadian farmer a preference in the markets of the United Kingdom."
HUGH JOHN MACDONALD—"I believe the first duty of a statesman is to respect his pledges to the people even to his own hurt."

Poster From the 1896 Election

Would They Win By A Nose?

Aware from the first that an election must be called before long, Tupper had already recruited star candidates to campaign. Almost the first thing he did as secretary of state was contact Robert Borden, who had become a party stalwart in Nova Scotia. At Tupper's request, Borden was a candidate in the election. For action in Québec, Tupper approached Adolphe Chapleau, a former federal cabinet minister as well as a former premier; but after four years of retirement, Chapleau was unwilling to stand for election again. Hugh Macdonald was more optimistic, and joined Cabinet as Minister of the Interior with goodwill. Hugh was not his father, and did not have Sir John A.'s political acumen, but still, his face and name were familiar. Posters were printed with both Tupper and Hugh Macdonald's names and faces, appealing to voter recognition. Predictions were made that the Tories would win – by a nose.

During the campaign, Tupper displayed determination and vigour in spite of his age, but he was still no match for the Liberals under Wilfrid Laurier, whose time had come. "Laurier was everything that Tupper was not," said a writer for the Canadian Encyclopedia. "Elegant and charming, he possessed a gift for finding compromise between apparently irreconcilable opponents."[9]

The Conservative party was not only disorganized, but had lost more public approval than it could afford. Some people called the party wasteful of public funds, and others considered the party corrupt with influence peddling and patronage appointments. Party members themselves were so divided over the Manitoba Schools question that Tupper faced criticism wherever he went on campaign, from Tories as well as Liberals.

Four days before the election, Tupper gave a two-hour speech at Massey Hall in Toronto, a stronghold of Tory support. But the audience showed mixed response as the Old Warhorse of Cumberland County approached the podium to speak. Conservative followers applauded Tupper, while Liberals in the crowd jeered loudly. Determined not to let himself be shouted down by the Liberal horde, Tupper waited, expressionless, some three or four minutes for the crowd to be quieter. When he finally began to talk, there were taunts throughout his speech. Any time Tupper referred to himself, the Liberals would holler "I, I, I" like hounds baying at the hunt. At any mention of the leader of the opposition, Wilfrid Laurier, the Liberals were on their feet, cheering. The interruptions were constant and so loud that, in the words of one journalist, "It was impossible to hear him, even at a distance of less than ten feet." Though fatigue and his age were taking their toll, Tupper didn't back down, condemning his critics with the words: "You men who are making these interruptions are the most block-headed set of cowards that I ever looked upon."[10]

Tupper and Lady Tupper 1896

A Lost Battle

It was clear as soon as the votes were counted that the Conservatives lost the election on June 23, 1896. The popular vote showed a surprising 48.2% for the Tories, but they took only 86 seats in the House of Commons while the Liberals under Laurier had 41.4% of the popular vote, but took 117 seats. Yet Tupper did not resign the office within a day, as is common practise in the 21st century. In fact, because the results were close enough for a recount in several ridings, he held onto power for two more weeks, while election results were appealed in several Québec ridings. During these last days in office, he was "determined to get approval for a few initiatives before stepping down, namely a new steamship line and raft of patronage appointments,"[11] for a long list of people he wished to appoint as senators and judges.

The Governor-General refused to sign those initiatives into law. Perhaps until then Tupper hadn't understood just how strong was Lord Aberdeen's dislike of patronage and of him as a person, to make this refusal absolute instead of accommodating the wishes of a retiring prime minister. To his surprise, Aberdeen was nobody he could dominate or persuade, unlike Lord Dufferin or Lord Lorne; Aberdeen remained confident that Tupper could no longer continue in the duties of prime minister. After spending his 75th birthday closeted with Lord Aberdeen, arguing his case with the Queen's representative,

Tupper was unsuccessful. He was also determined not to retire, though he did have to resign the reins of power to Laurier. Two days later, on July 8, 1896, Tupper formally resigned his term as Canada's sixth prime minister – and the one with the briefest term ever, at only sixty-nine days.

Stubbornly, he refused to retire from politics. Having been elected, he served as the MP for Cumberland County. Since he led the Conservative Party, he served in the House as the leader of the Opposition. Sir Wilfrid Laurier had led the Liberals to victory, and was to remain prime minister until 1911, winning an unprecedented four elections in a row.

It appears that Lord Aberdeen was not the only person who disapproved of patronage appointments – or perhaps the appointing of people whose performance was less effective than expected. Shortly after the election of 1896, some of Tupper's patronage appointments were abruptly reversed by Laurier as the new prime minister, even some appointments of long standing. Royal Military College at Kingston was suddenly no longer commanded by Tupper's son-in-law Donald Cameron. Though he'd been commanding the college since 1888, Cameron was a weak commandant and wasn't considered to have been assigned the position on his own merit. When the Liberals came to power in 1896, they turfed him out and appointed a new commandant.

Emma Cameron had put down some roots in Kingston during their eight years there, active in programs supporting the poor and homeless. She and Donald Cameron settled in a fine home at Bexley Heath in North Kent, England. In 1901, her parents would come to live there as well.

Tupper in Profile

A Unique Prime Minister

When Tupper took office at the age of 74 years and 304 days, he became the oldest person to take office as a prime minister of Canada. A hundred and twenty years later, he is still the oldest. When he conceded losing the election of 1896, he was only a few days older than Donald Trump would be in 2020 when he lost the American election for the presidency.

His longevity is notable in other ways. When he passed away, it was at the age of 94 years and 120 days, older even than Mackenzie Bowell. No other prime minister has come close to living this long.

Tupper was perhaps the only prime minister of Canada who never served as a Member of Parliament or Senator during any point of his tenure as prime minister. He had been an MP before, representing Cumberland from 1867 – 1884, and again from 1887 – 1888, when he resigned his seat to eliminate a conflict of interest in his post as High Commissioner. During the 1896 election he won a seat and served as an MP again for four years, representing Cape Breton till 1900. But during the months from January to May 1896 when he was secretary of state, and from May 1 to July 8 while he was in office as prime minister during the election, Tupper was not actually sworn in for either the Senate or the House of Commons.

John Turner would later become the only other prime minister who might not have been sworn in as a Member of Parliament or Senator during his tenure as prime minister. He was not an MP when the Liberal party called on him to serve out the end of Pierre Trudeau's term after Trudeau retired. Author David Blake, however, reports that Turner was sworn in as member for Vancouver Quadra riding a short while before he resigned as prime minister. Tupper did not have any such hasty swearing-in. Perhaps he felt as bound as he ever was by his previous oaths. At any rate, he was far too busy during the campaign for an election the Conservatives lost.

1 Hammond, M.O. Canadian Confederation and its Leaders. New York, NY: G.H. Doran, May, 1917. Electric Canadian website. Retrieved June 10, 2015. http://www.electriccanadian.com/makers/confederation/chapter15.htm

2 House of Commons Debates, Official Report, Volume 2. June 17, 1887, p1098.

3 House of Commons Debates, Official Report, Volume 2. June 17, 1887, p1107.

4 Editorial. "Contagious Pleuro-Pneumonia and the Canadian Cattle Trade." The British Veterinary Journal and Annals of Comparative Pathology, Volume 37. London, UK: Hazell, Watson and Viney Ltd., 1893. pp 255-259.

5 "Tupper, Sir Charles." Dictionary of Canadian Biography. Retrieved March 20, 2016. http://www.biographi.ca/en/bio/tupper_charles_14E.html

6 Hammond, op.cit.

7 Hammond, op.cit.

8 Shields, R.A. "Sir Charles Tupper and the Franco-Canadian Treaty of 1895: A Study of Imperial Relations." The Canadian Historical Review, Vol. XLIX, #1, March 1968. Toronto, ON: University of Toronto Press. Retrieved June 26, 2016. http://dx.doi.org/10.3138/CHR-049-01-01

9 Azzi, Stephen. "The Election of 1896." Historica Canada. Updated February 9, 2015. Retrieved July 4, 2016. http://www.thecanadianencyclopedia.ca/en/article/election-1896-feature/

10 Azzi, ibid.

11 Sclee, Gary. "Tupper gives up the battle." Canadian Prime Ministers. Posted July 8, 2016. Retrieved July 15, 2016. https://canadianprimeministers.wordpress.com/2016/07/08/tupper-gives-up-the-battle/

Chapter 8: Tupper's Conservative Legacy

THE END OF TUPPER'S brief term as prime minister was not the end of his life, nor his political career. He was active in Opposition for four years, and afterwards continued a busy schedule managing investments. Even in retirement, he was still writing and learning and travelling in his nineties. Only weeks before his death, he was still an influence on the current prime minister of Canada.

The Tupper Family 1896

His Last Years in the House

As Leader of the Opposition, Tupper was fiercely active, and worked hard to rebuild his party's influence. For all parties in central Canada there was renewed interest in the Northwest Territories, because of the 1896 discovery of gold in a tributary of the Klondike River. In addition to speaking on this and other topics in the House, Tupper kept up an impressive schedule for four years touring the country coast-to-coast, and visiting England for a month or more twice a year. Frequently, he would deliver two or three talks a day to various community groups while staying as the guest of provincial premiers and lieutenant-governors. During all his travels, he was accompanied by his wife Frances and a granddaughter or two. Of course, he made sure to bring them to glamourous events in London during Queen Victoria's Diamond Jubilee in 1897.

The Tuppers were among the "boatloads of colonial politicians" in London for the celebration. "It is hard to determine if any came with the express purpose of turning a quick profit at the expense of credulous British investors, but a suspiciously large number of prominent western Canadians were listed in the prospectuses of mining companies issued in 1897 and 1898," noted writer Jeremy Mouat, adding that "Tupper chaired New Goldfields of British Columbia and the Klondyke Mining, Trading and Transport Corporation. ...The grandiosely styled British Empire Finance Corporation was a condominium company with Sir Charles Tupper representing Canada and a handful of Western Australian politicians adding further colonial lustre to the corporate image."[1]

Mouat quotes a contemporary's observation that a charter for trading and mining in the Yukon district could be bought for a million pounds (some $5 million), but anyone unable to come up with the whole might be glad to take advantage of aggregate financing, sharing both the cost and the risk of the investment. Finding investors was a particular talent that Tupper had perfected after years of networking, and he could persuade people to support his projects. "He was a director in a British-financed firm, the New Gold Fields company which had bought out the Klondike Mining, Trading and Transportation Company, which in turn had tentative plans to build a railway [to Yukon Territory] between Portland Canal and Teslin Lake,"[2] noted historian D.J. Hall, quoting not only the Globe newspaper from 1897 but a letter from Tupper to his son Charles Hibbert in August of 1897.

The purpose of all this travel was to promote projects he felt were in Canada's best interest, including such things as new steamship companies and mining corporations. How would the border be set between Alaska and Canada? Both Tupper and his son Sir Charles Hibbert Tupper spoke at length in Canada's House of Commons about the International Commission that had still not settled the disputed border. This issue grew more important when a gold rush began in the summer of 1897, which saw some 100,000 people flock to the region, most passing through the disputed border en route.

Both the elder and younger Tupper took turns addressing the House with seven-hour speeches supporting the formation of Yukon Territory, to be administered separately from the rest of the Northwest Territories. They sorely tried the patience of fellow MPs and transcribers for Hansard. As well, Tupper tried to use the international issue of the Boer War to undermine the Liberal government, to no avail.

Outside of Parliament, Tupper used his influence to help two friends in Montréal who were starting a French-language newspaper. Subscribers were found, so that this paper could be supported without relying too much on advertising. Communications media was an expanding market.

At this time, there were thirty ships laying telegraph cables across ocean floors around the world, twenty-four of them owned by British companies determined to link all the British Empire; in 1898 Tupper supported the laying of cables connecting Canada to the Far East. By 1902, telegraph cables would connect Canada's Vancouver Island to Fanning Island, and even to Australia via other islands in the South Pacific. The "All Red Route" linking the British Empire and former British colonies (all shown in red on British maps) was becoming a world-wide web of telegraph cables, promoted by Tupper and other supporters of communication services.

Tupper and Hugh Macdonald

Misstep in Manitoba

In 1900, a federal election was called. This became Tupper's last campaign. As was always his practise before and during elections, he attended every meeting he could, campaigning for the benefit of other candidates as well as himself. He was all of 79 years old, and must have been feeling his age by the time the votes were cast.

Unfortunately, when the election had not yet been called, Tupper's work to support Hugh Macdonald's chances backfired. While in Brandon, Manitoba at a debate in 1899, Tupper spoke condemning Clifford Sifton, a lawyer running as a Liberal in the same riding as Hugh Macdonald. Tupper accused Sifton of permitting "his former partner, Brandon lawyer A.E. Philp, to import liquor illegally into the Yukon."[3] The accusation made a sensation. "Sifton then had promptly denounced Tupper's statement as a lie, and Philp had sued Sir Charles for libel."[4]

Actually, in all his patronage appointments Sifton had been careful not to employ his relatives, nor did he find jobs for party supporters who were not qualified. "Political patronage was generally accepted as a stabilizing element in the political process in this pre-war era; political corruption was not,"[5] noted historian W. Leland Clark.

During the 1900 election campaign, the younger Tupper was set to debate Sifton in Brandon, and repeated his father's accusation. Unfortunately, only a few days before that debate the elder Tupper had reluctantly consented to making an unconditional withdrawal of the charge and an apology. This news made a sensation when released at the debate. "Sifton triumphantly read the correspondence to the astonished crowd," noted writer D.J. Hall. In an era with no telephones and limited availability of telegraphs for personal use, at this public debate not even Tupper's son had heard yet of the settlement. Hall went on to quote Sifton as saying "'Those of you who were here last year and heard Sir Charles Tupper upon the platform and heard him make that charge -—will realize the depth of the humiliation of that gentleman in signing a complete, absolute recantation.' ...Liberal organizers were delightedly claiming that the meeting had gained one hundred votes for the government side, and they may have been right. Certainly it was a blow from which Macdonald's campaign never recovered."[6] Young Macdonald didn't win the seat, and neither did Tupper win his own seat, though Sir Charles Hibbert Tupper did.

"Defeat doubtless came to him as a relief, for on election night he bade his circle of friends in Halifax to be of good cheer," wrote historian Hammond, adding that Tupper told them: "Do not let a trifling matter like this interfere with the pleasures of a social evening." It seems Tupper took this election defeat as his cue to retire, and that he did so with a calm mind. His journal entry for that day ended with the words "I went to bed and slept soundly."[7]

Two weeks after the election, Tupper resigned his roles as Leader of the Opposition and leader of the Conservative Party of Canada. For his successor, the caucus chose Robert Borden, also from Nova Scotia. With that choice, Tupper was well content. He had served four prime ministers, and now he had helped his party to choose a leader who he knew well from Borden's law partnership with his sons. He had a son active in Parliament. It was time to retire.

After the election defeat in 1900, Tupper retired from politics. He was willing to listen to praise of his governments' actions on taxes, expenditure and public debt, but not to praise about himself. "Now, that will never do my man; you will make me conceited, you will give me a swelled head, and that is a bad thing for a public man."[8]

Tupper at a meeting of the directors of the Crown Life Insurance Co. In Toronto, circa 1900

Investment Anecdote

In his mature years and after retirement, Tupper made money investing in railroad stocks. It was an investment that made good sense, as railways were expanding in many routes through Canada and the USA. But on at least one occasion his investment missed a golden opportunity. In 1901, Tupper picked up 250 shares of Northern Pacific Railway stock at 100 1/2. He then travelled to Europe. While returning to Canada from Britain, he received telegrams from friends and family notifying him that Northern Pacific was having incredible price improvements, from $125 to about $400 a share. It went to $1000 a share on May 4th.

Unfortunately, all the paperwork for Tupper's stocks was locked in a strongbox in Canada. It was safe, but also unable to be sold by any of his friends or relatives. He had not given anyone power of attorney. That was a surprising error for a man eighty years old on good terms with his younger family members.

The next day, the stock's prices returned to $150 a share. He landed at the wharf to learn that his failure to appoint an attorney in his absence had cost him over $200,000. In 1901, this was an immense fortune. Yet, he didn't appear to lose any sleep over the issue. In fact, he told the story with enthusiasm.

1901 was a year of many changes for investments based in Britain or Canada. Several of the smaller mining companies and a few of the larger ones went bankrupt and were unable to pay creditors, even after liquidating all assets.

Tupper Stamp

Retirement in England

1901 was also the year Sir Charles and Lady Tupper retired to England, living at their estate in Bexley Heath in north-west Kent. Their daughter Emma Cameron and granddaughter Marie Tupper (daughter of their eldest son) managed the home.

Despite his advancing age, Tupper continued to make regular trips back to Canada. Twenty-seven years after his first visit to British Columbia, Tupper toured the city of Vancouver, admiring the new buildings in the business district. He commented to his associate Saunders: "I well remember that when passing through the forest in 1881, about where we now stand, the luxuriant ferns growing under the great trees waved about my horse's head."[9]

His primary reason to cross the Atlantic was to visit his sons. Both J. Stewart Tupper and William Johnston Tupper were still practising law in Winnipeg – the eldest had become a member of Queen's Counsel and had built a large mansion. As for William, he became a member of King's Counsel in 1913, and began his political career in 1914. Between visiting his lawyer sons and his middle son (now Sir Charles Hibbert Tupper) who remained active in federal politics, there were many reasons bringing Tupper back to Canada for visits.

These years of retirement were not an idle time for Tupper. Even in his 80s, Tupper remained active in British and imperial politics. He was made a member of the British Privy Council on November 9, 1907. As well, he was promoted to the rank of Knight Grand Cross of the Order of St Michael and St George, which entitled him to use the letters "GCMG" after his name. Tupper took a particular interest in promoting Canada's place within the British Empire. Though some commentators believed there was no future for the Empire but a federation of all its colonies, Tupper supported the idea of a looser association something like the Commonwealth which has emerged.

By the age of 84, Tupper's health was declining. Even so, he took an opportunity to visit Rome and begin the study of the Italian language.

With the death of Lady Frances in May 1912, Tupper felt her loss and his own age keenly. He had her body returned to Canada, and buried her in Halifax. At last he wrote his memoirs, and gave a series of interviews to a journalist which were the basis of another book.

The marriage of Frances and Charles Tupper was the longest-lasting marriage made by any Canadian prime minister. They had already been married forty-eight years when he took office, a timespan longer than the life expectancy for the average person born when they were. By the time of Frances's death, they had been married for sixty-six years.

Failing Health

In April of 1915, Tupper's eldest son died. It's hard for any father to outlive a son, and in Tupper's case, this loss was a crippling blow for the last months of his life. During World War I, by 1915 Tupper had three grandsons fighting on the front lines. Charles Stewart Tupper, son of Tupper's eldest son, served as a Captain in the Queen's Own Cameron Highlanders. He was at Ypres in 1916, having inherited his grandfather's title as Baronet of Armdale, and returned to Winnipeg after the war. Victor Gordon Tupper, son of his middle son, served as a Captain in a Manitoba regiment, and died at Vimy Ridge in 1917. James Tupper, son of his middle son, was a barber conscripted to service who died in 1919.

Even in the last year of his life, Tupper was still alert and canny, though mellowing with age. He continued correspondence with the current prime minister of Canada, Sir Robert Borden. While Borden was visiting Europe, reviewing Canadian troops during the First World War, he made sure to visit Tupper at Bexley Heath.[10] It was their last meeting, and the last opportunity they had for political machinations. Not even six weeks passed before Tupper had a heart attack, and it was clear that his life was winding down. A month later, Tupper passed away in his sleep on October 30, 1915.

At his death, he was the last surviving Father of Confederation, and he had become the longest-living Canadian prime minister, at the age of 94 years and four months. There was very probably a genetic factor contributing to Tupper's long life. Several of his grandchildren lived to be over eighty years old. His first grandchild was almost a hundred years old at her death.

He wasn't the only prime minister to die on the 30th of October. John Abbott, who was born the same year as Tupper, resigned his own term as prime minister because of ill health. On October 30 1893 he died of stomach cancer. Twenty-two years later, Tupper died of heart failure.

His body was brought back to Canada on HMS Blenheim, the same ship which returned the body of Sir John Thompson to Halifax after Thompson's sudden death in England 1894. At his state funeral there was a mile-long procession, and then Tupper was buried in Halifax in St John's Cemetery beside the grave of his wife Frances.

Tupper in Old Age

His Legacy

Making an accurate assessment of a Canadian politician after the fact is a tough task. There's the matter of "reverse perspective," as political scientist David Smith called the fact that influential people seem to grow larger the farther away in time they are from the present day. Smith believed as well that it was impossible to make fair comparisons among Canadian prime ministers. He felt they had little in common and were far from a set of equals. The prime ministers who were in office during Tupper's years in politics were certainly different from each other, though all worked to lead their political parties.

The impression that Tupper has left as a prime minister, among Canadian historians, is not much better than that of Bowell. He is generally ranked as a failure, or at best a place-holder who was not able to keep that office secure for the coming election. Certainly he looks like a failure compared to Laurier who took office in that election, and held it for four terms.

It's not hard for any prime minister to look like a failure when compared to Laurier! Many commentators consider Laurier the finest prime minister Canada has had. A survey of Canadian historians was made in 1999, asking them to rank the 20 prime ministers who had so far held office. When the results were counted, Laurier was number one. Tupper was ranked at 16th of the 20 because of his very short tenure in office.

To be better than the worst – that's not a ringing endorsement. It is difficult to accomplish much of significance in an administration that was largely taken up by one issue and an election campaign. The issue which drove that election – the Manitoba Schools Question – was addressed in one of Laurier's first acts as prime minister. The solution he implemented was a compromise, stating that Catholics in Manitoba could have a Catholic education, on a school-by-school basis if there were enough students to warrant it. This compromise bore similarity to Tupper's education legislation thirty years earlier in Nova Scotia.

As a prime minister, Tupper was one of what Francine McKenzie termed "ancillary" prime ministers. Other analysts consider these four successors of Macdonald to be "caretaker" prime ministers, and this term is more accurate. The hapless successors of Sir John A. Macdonald tried in vain to hold together the Conservative party as a governing power, but did not have the patience and imagination of Macdonald.

While Tupper was a failure as a prime minister, he was a success as a career politician. Tupper worked for party unity among the Conservatives in the face of strong regional loyalties. He is worth remembering more for his decades of work as a member of Parliament and a High Commissioner than for his few weeks as a prime minister. He worked for decades as part of the government of "a country notable for the tensions thrown up by a precarious national sentiment, a powerful and not always sympathetic neighbour, and cultural duality,"[11] wrote historian Blair Neatby. as quoted in Maclean's magazine.

Though his work best served Conservatives and corporate executives, to an extent that went beyond partisan support to acts of patronage and influence peddling that would be condemned in the 21st century, Tupper didn't see that as wrong. He thought his party held itself responsible for the needs of citizens.

He felt a particular responsibility for the people of Nova Scotia. In his opinion, corporations and private businessmen developed natural resources to support the economy.

And though this development and responsibility came at the expense of First Nations people, particularly in the Western Provinces, he didn't see that as wrong. Though he worked to encourage Catholics and Protestants to get along, and French and English-speaking citizens, Tupper did not support the interests of First Nations as citizens. He represented the interests of the new country Canada nationally and internationally, even when these interests conflicted with those of America, or Britain, or First Nations.

By the time of Tupper's death, Laurier was able to eulogise him in positive terms, if not glowing praise. "In my judgment," said Sir Wilfrid Laurier in 1916, "the chief characteristic of Tupper was courage; courage which no obstacle could down, which rushed to the assault, and which, if repulsed, came back to the combat again and again; courage which battered and hammered, perhaps not always judiciously, but always effectively; courage which never admitted defeat, and which in the midst of overwhelming disaster ever maintained the proud carriage of unconquerable defiance."[12]

In the last year of Tupper's life, a bronze sign was put on display in the Charlottetown building where the Fathers of Confederation first assembled. The news was sent to Tupper in his retirement, and he read the words preserved there:

"Unity is strength. In the hearts and minds of the delegates who assembled in this room in September 1, 1864, was born the Dominion of Canada. Providence being their guide, they builded better than they knew. This tablet erected on the occasion of the fiftieth anniversary of the event."[13]

1 Mouat, Jeremy. *Roaring Days: Rossland's Mines and the History of British Columbia.* p54.

2 Hall, D.J. *Clifford Sifton, Volume 1: The Young Napoleon, 1861-1900.* p299.

3 Clark, W. Landon. *Brandon's Politics and Politicians.* Brandon, MB: Brandon Sun, 1981, p.18. http://www.mhs.mb.ca/docs/books/brandonpolitics.pdf

4 Hall, D.J. *Clifford Sifton, Volume 1: The Young Napoleon, 1861-1900.* p329.

5 Clark, ibid.

6 Hall, D.J. op.cit. p.329.

7 Hammond, M.O. *Canadian Confederation and its Leaders*. New York,NY: G.H. Doran, May, 1917. Electric Canadian website. Retrieved June 10, 2015. http://www.electriccanadian.com/makers/confederation/chapter15.htm

8 Saunders, E.M., editor. *The Life and Letters of the Rt. Hon. Sir Charles Tupper, Bart., K.C.M.G.* Toronto, ON: Cassell and Co. 1916.

9 Saunders, op.cit., p 313.

10 Schlee, Gary. "Borden meets Tupper at Bexley Heath." *Canadian Prime Ministers*. Posted August 14, 2009. Retrieved November 20, 2015. https://canadianprimeministers.wordpress.com/2009/08/14/borden-meets-tupper-at-bexley-heath/

11 Norman Hillmer and J.L. Granatstein. "Historians rank the BEST AND WORST Canadian Prime Ministers." *Maclean's* magazine. April 21, 1997. Retrieved January 26, 2016. http://www.ggower.com/dief/text/maclean2.shtml

12 Hammond, op. cit.

13 Letter of Bartlett to Tupper, October 14, 1914, Letter 1169, Tupper Papers, Public Archives of Canada.

Glossary

anthrax - a disease, often fatal, which can be caught by inhaling or eating spores, or through breaks in the skin.

24 Sussex Drive - the official residence in Ottawa for the leader of the governing party in the House of Commons.

cabinet minister - a member of the legislature, either in the House of Commons or more rarely the Senate, who has been asked by the prime minister to lead a government department or ministry of state. The cabinet acts as a team to manage the federal government.

CBC - The Canadian Broadcasting Corporation, known as Radio Canada in French; the national broadcasting company with both radio and television programming available across the country, including the far North, and world-wide on the Internet and on shortwave radio as Radio Canada International until that program was shut down by the Harper government.

Canadian Constitution - the set of laws dictating how the government in Canada is expected to govern the country. Though first passed in 1867 in Great Britain, the constitution was patriated under Canadian law in 1982 under Prime Minister Pierre Trudeau.

Canadian Medical Association - Formed in 1867, this professional organization acts to set standards for the quality of medical doctors. Charles Tupper was the founding president for a three-year term.

Canadian Pacific Railway - the first transcontinental railway in Canada. From 1882 – 1885, tracks were laid between Montréal and Vancouver. By 1889, tracks reached Saint John, NB by veering through the American state of Maine.

chief medical officer - a qualified physician whose duty is advising on public health issues rather than treating individual patients. Some responsibilities include creating health programs to prevent illness or to reduce the spread of infectious diseases.

colonies - groups of people living in a territory, governed by laws of an administrative country. England had several colonies in North America and other places around the world.

Confederation - the union of provinces or states as one country. Each member state or province is partly self-governing, but some government responsibilities are administered centrally for all members.

Conservative Party - a national party which has roots dating back to Britain's Parliament and the Tories.

diphtheria - a respiratory disease spread by contact with particles from sneezing or coughing.

dowry - a traditional gift of land, money, or other valuables that a bride brings to her marriage. It was her birth family's contribution to the expense of setting up a new household.

Governor-General - a representative of the British crown in Canada appointed for a five-year term. A governor-general signs into law all the acts passed by Parliament, giving them royal assent, acting as our nation's head of state. The role is formal and ceremonial, but has become almost entirely symbolic. Since 1867, Rideau Hall in Ottawa has been the home and workplace for every governor general.

High Commissioner - a senior diplomat appointed by one country to be a representative in another country. Unlike an ambassador, a High Commissioner is usually appointed to deal with a particular time-sensitive issue.

House of Commons - Within Canada's Parliament, the House of Commons includes members who are elected by the citizens to represent small areas in each province or territory. These members may be independent, but most belong to an official party. The largest party or alliance of parties in the House forms the government, selecting a cabinet of ministers to manage government departments and ministries. The cabinet is led by a prime minister, who selects the Speaker presiding over meetings of the House. Members who are not in the governing party are considered the opposition parties. All new laws start by being read and debated in the House before being signed by Cabinet, read and debated in the Senate, and finally signed into law by the governor general.

influenza - a respiratory disease spread by contact with particles from sneezing or coughing. Before the discovery of germs, this disease was thought to be "influenced" by bad air and storms.

Liberal Party - a national party with roots dating back to Britain's Parliament and the Whigs. Canada's Liberal party was formed after Confederation in 1867, from a union of the Reform party in the province of Ontario and the Parti rouge in the province of Québec.

Lower Canada (1791 – 1840) - the Constitutional act of 1791 divided the Province of Québec into Upper Canada and Lower Canada. In 1841 the provinces were reunited as the Province of Canada. After Confederation in 1867, Canada West became known as Ontario, and Canada East became known as Québec.

majority government - when the party with the most seats in the House of Commons has more seats than the other parties put together.

Manitoba Schools Question - an issue debated in Parliament about whether Manitoba should have a publicly funded Catholic school system in addition to the public schools (which had a minimal amount of religious content in a daily Protestant prayer). At the province's formation in 1879, both school systems were run by the provincial government.

Maritimes - a region on the North Atlantic coast of North America including the British colonies which became the provinces of Nova Scotia, New Brunswick, and Prince Edward Island. In the 21st century, the Maritime provinces are sometimes considered informally to include as well the province of Newfoundland and Labrador, though that crown colony did not join Confederation until 1949.

minority government - when the party with the most seats in the House of Commons is outnumbered by the seats held by other parties.

MP - an elected member of the House of Commons in Canada's Parliament.

Parliament - the representatives of Canada's federal government; the House of Commons is filled with members of Parliament who have been elected by Canadians, and the Senate is filled with senators appointed by the prime minister.

responsible government - a government managed by a legislature of representatives elected by citizens, which is independent of a colonial authority such as Britain, in contrast to a colonial government which may have an elected legislature but their colonial governor administrates authority for Britain.

scarlatina or scarlet fever - an infectious disease caused by Streptococcus bacteria, resulting a sore throat, rash, and high fever. Complications include rheumatic fever, kidney damage, and death.

vote of confidence - when a vote is called on a bill of great importance in the House of Commons, usually on a budget; if the bill is defeated the House is said to have lost confidence in the governing party, and an election is usually called.

Persons of Interest

Abbott, John Joseph Caldwell (1821 – 1893) Third Prime Minister of Canada, and the first born in Canada, he served for seventeen months from June 16, 1891, to November 24, 1892 before resigning in favour of John Thompson.

Aberdeen, Lady (1857 – 1939) Born Ishbel Maria Marjoribanks. Wife of Lord Aberdeen. She was an activist promoting women's rights and increased roles in society for women. In Canada, she founded the National Council of Women and the Victorian Order of Nurses.

Aberdeen, Lord (1847 – 1934) Born John Campbell Hamilton Gordon, in Edinburgh, Scotland, the son of a prime minister of England. Canada's seventh governor general (1893 – 1898). Resident in Canada only during his term in office.

Big Bear (1825 – 1888) Ojibwe/Cree leader of a First Nations alliance in what is now the province of Saskatchewan. He recommended a large reserve protecting a major portion of the Prairies instead of the small, scattered reserves preferred by the Canadian government. In 1876 he signed a treaty that ceded traditional lands, under duress, only because his people were starving; the vast herds of bison they relied on had been exterminated under government orders (as noted in *Clearing the Plains* by James Daschuk). Though he worked for peace during the 1885 Rebellion he was jailed afterwards.

Borden, Sir Robert (1854 – 1937) Canada's eighth prime minister (1911 – 1920). Born in Nova Scotia, Borden worked as a teacher and later became a lawyer. In 1896, he entered politics as a member of the Conservative party. In the 1911 election he led the Conservatives to victory, defeating Laurier's Liberal government.

Bowell, Sir Mackenzie (1823 – 1917) Canada's fifth prime minister (December 12, 1894 – April 27, 1896). Born in England. During his short term, Bowell attempted to re-establish in 1895 Manitoba's separate school system for Catholic students.

Bulwer-Lytton, Baron Edward (1803 – 1873) British secretary of state for the colonies during Tupper's first visits to London representing Nova Scotia. Lytton is better remembered as the author of a potboiler novel which opened with the words, "It was a dark and stormy night..."

Cameron, Donald Roderick (1837-1921) Husband of Tupper's daughter Emma. Born in Scotland, he was a Captain of the Royal Artillery in 1856 and fought in the Bhutan Campaign in India (1864-1865). Though not distinguished as assistant to William McDowell in his role at Red River Settlement in 1869, with recommendations from Tupper and Sir John A. Macdonald, Cameron served later as commissioner on the British-American boundary survey from 1872 to 1876, managing the British section. He was also secretary of the Canadian delegation at the Paris Conference on Submarine Cables in 1883, as well as secretary to the Canadian Commission on Fisheries in Washington in 1887-88. It was certainly with Tupper's influence that Cameron commanded the Royal Military College in Kingston from 1888-1896, as that position was ended when Tupper lost the 1896 election.

Cartier, George-Étienne (1814 – 1873) A politician from Lower Canada (now called Québec). From 1857 – 1862, Cartier was co-premier of the Province of Canada with John A. Macdonald. With Macdonald, he worked to unite the British colonies in North America. Considered a Father of Confederation, he served in the first coalition cabinet as defence minister. Often he replaced Macdonald at the duties of prime minister in the House of Commons.

Cartier, Jacques (1491 – 1557) A French-born explorer who made three voyages to North America in 1534, 1535, and 1541. Searching for a passage to China, Cartier made it no further than the Lachine rapids on the St Lawrence river at Montréal.

Chipman, Clarence Campbell (1856 – 1924) Born in Amherst NS, Chipman joined the civil service. He worked as a private secretary for Tupper from 1882 to 1888 and then for his son Charles Hibbert Tupper. From 1891 to 1912 he was a commissioner for the HBC, supervising the efficient streamlining of management and promoting economy.

Connolly, Thomas Louis (1814 – 1876) Born in Cork, Ireland, Connolly became a Capuchin monk, priest, and served in Nova Scotia, becoming Archbishop of Halifax in 1858. His tolerance and moderation did much to calm religious unrest over education, the Gourley Riots, and enlistment in wars overseas. He became a strong supporter of confederation and a long-time correspondent of both Tupper and Sir John A. Macdonald. He worked to heal the rift between those supporting and those against Confederation, and between Catholics and Protestants over the Fenian troubles.

Fathers of Confederation – Thirty-six delegates from provincial parliaments, who represented the British North American colonies at three conferences between 1864 and 1867 in Charlottetown, Québec, and London. Together they fostered the Confederation of Canada.

Fenian Brotherhood – An American radical group of Irish immigrants. The Fenians spoke out in favour of invading British colonies and taking control until their demands were met. When Great Britain returned control of Ireland back to the Irish, the Fenians would return control of the colonies to Britain. Their raids into Canada East and Canada West in 1866 and 1870 were unsuccessful. Their attempted 1871 raid into Manitoba was foiled when Louis Riel and Ambroise Lépine rallied the Métis in Red River to support Manitoba's new Lieutenant-Governor Archibald, and American soldiers captured the Fenians at Pembina on the border.

Howe, Joseph (1804 – 1873) Born in Halifax, Nova Scotia, Howe became a controversial journalist and then entered politics as a Liberal. Campaigning against Confederation, he led the opposition forces. A political opponent of Tupper, he nonetheless joined a federal coalition cabinet when Tupper recruited him.

Hudson's Bay Company (incorporated 1670 – present) Founded in 1670 England to trade in furs with First Nations people in North America. In practise, the company managed all the lands draining into Hudson Bay, a huge area that became known as Rupert's Land, extending from Labrador across Ungava Québec and Ontario, and west of Lake Superior across the Prairies to the Rocky Mountains, including a swath of land south of what became the border between Canada and the United States. The company changed in the 20th century, and is now a chain of retail stores called simply "The Bay."

Johnston, James William – (1792 – 1893) A lawyer who became premier of the colony of Nova Scotia for three terms, from 1844 – 1848, 1857 – 1859, and 1863 – 1864. He was instrumental in ending a coal monopoly in Nova Scotia that had seen one company control all the coal production until 1857. On his appointment to be a judge in 1864, Johnston gave up leadership of the Conservative party in Nova Scotia, passing that role on to Charles Tupper.

Laurier, Sir Wilfrid (1841 – 1911) Canada's seventh prime minister, and the first of French-Canadian descent. In his first term, Laurier implemented a solution to the Manitoba Schools question which had helped bring down the Conservative government under Charles Tupper in 1896.

Lowe, Miriam Mother of Charles Tupper. Born Miriam Lowe, her first marriage brought her the name Lockheart and six children. Her second marriage, to Reverend Tupper, brought her five more children including Charles.

Macdonald, Sir John A. (1815 – 1891) Born in Scotland, Macdonald moved with his parents to Upper Canada in 1820. He became a lawyer before entering politics. For many years, his goal was to bring the Province of Canada together with the Maritime provinces. Confederation in 1867 saw this goal realised. Macdonald was appointed Canada's first prime minister, to lead a coalition cabinet with members from both parties. He served two terms as prime minister, from 1867 – 1873 and 1878 – 1891.

Macdonald, Susan Agnes Bernard (1835 – 1920) The second wife of Sir John A. Macdonald, married in February 1867. Noted for riding a CP Rail train, on the cowcatcher, as it passed through the Rockies. After her husband's death in 1891, she moved with their only daughter to England.

Mackenzie, Alexander (1822 – 1892) Liberal party leader and the second prime minister of Canada. A stonemason by trade, Mackenzie was the only early prime minister to turn down a knighthood.

McDougall, William (1822 – 1905) Served as minister of public works in Sir John A. Macdonald's first cabinet, where he managed the purchase of Rupert's Land from the Hudson's Bay Company. Afterwards, McDougall was appointed lieutenant-governor of the newly-named Northwest Territories of Canada, but he was prevented by the Provisional Government of Red River from entering the Territories.

McGee, Thomas D'Arcy (1825 – 1868) Born in Ireland, McGee became a journalist, poet, and politician in Canada. He was elected to the Legislative Assembly of the Province of Canada, serving from

1857 – 1867. A Father of Confederation, he was a member of the first Canadian Parliament. In his youth, McGee campaigned for Ireland's independence from Great Britain. Later, the critical comments he published concerning the Irish independence movement and the Fenians probably contributed to his assassination.

Morse, Frances Amelia (1826 – 1912) Born in Amherst, Nova Scotia, Morse married Tupper on October 8, 1846. She bore their children, including three daughters, two of whom died as infants, and three sons. She kept home for their family in Nova Scotia and Ottawa, and in Bexley Heath, England.

New England Planters (arrival in Nova Scotia 1759-1768) Eight thousand settlers from New England colonies, who accepted the invitations of Nova Scotia governor Charles Lawrence to settle lands that were left vacant after the 1755 Bay of Fundy Campaign during the expulsion of the Acadians. Though they were later outnumbered by United Empire Loyalists who came after the American War of Independence in 1783, Planters laid the foundation for communities and culture in Nova Scotia and the newly-partitioned colony of New Brunswick.

Riel, Louis (1844 – 1885) Canada's most controversial historical figure. Born a Métis in Red River Settlement, Riel was trained in Montréal for the priesthood and as a teacher and a lawyer, but left those callings and returned to Red River. In the settlement's provisional government of 1869-70, he quickly emerged as a leader. It is fair to call him a father of Confederation, as he took Tupper's advice and negotiated the entry of Manitoba into Confederation in 1870, and in 1884 was called on by the Métis community in Saskatchewan to negotiate for them with the government of Canada. When the North West Rebellion was defeated, Riel was tried for high treason and hanged after a controversial trial.

Stewart, Alexander (1794 – 1865) Uncle of Frances Morse. He was a lawyer and represented Cumberland County as a Liberal in Nova Scotia's House of Assembly from 1826 – 1838. Later, he was appointed to be a judge.

Thompson, Sir John Sparrow David (1845 – 1894) The fourth prime minister of Canada, and the first who was Roman Catholic. He was instrumental in creating Canada's first criminal code, which gave power to the federal government to prosecute criminal offences.

Timeline

July 2, 1821 Birth of Charles Tupper at the family farm near Amherst, Nova Scotia

Education:

1836 apprenticeship with Dr Benjamin Page in Amherst, NS

August 1837 entered Horton Academy in Wolfville, NS

1839-40 studied medicine as an apprentice under Dr Ebenezer Fitch Harding of Windsor, NS.

1840-43 attended University of Edinburgh, Scotland to earn a medical degree

April 20, 1843 Graduated from the Royal College of Surgeons of Edinburgh

1843 opened his medical practise in Cumberland County, NS

October 8, 1846 Married Frances Amelia Morse

Their Children:

Emma Tupper (1847–1925)

Elizabeth Stewart (Lillie) Tupper (April–November 1849)

James Orrin Stewart Tupper (October 21, 1851–April 29, 1915) – lawyer, QC

Charles Hibbert Tupper (August 3, 1855–March 30, 1927) – Tory MP for Pictou, NS

Sophy Almon Tupper (1858–1863)

William Johnston Tupper (June 29, 1862—December 17, 1947) – Manitoba MLA for Winnipeg, lieutenant-governor for Manitoba 1934-40

1855 entered politics as a Conservative with the election in Nova Scotia

From 1855 until Confederation in 1867, elected in Cumberland County as a member of the legislative assembly of the Colony of Nova Scotia

1864 became premier of Nova Scotia on the resignation of William Johnston

1867 Confederation of Canada, for which he was knighted by Queen Victoria appointed to represent Cumberland County, NS in Canada's Parliament

1867 declined a seat in the Canadian Cabinet

1868 declined the chairmanship of intercolonial railway board

June 1870 to July 1872 president of privy council (federal cabinet)

July 1872 to February 1873 minister of inland revenue

February 1873 to November 1873 minister of customs

November 1873 to 1878 in Opposition, shadow to the Liberals' minister of finance

Summers 1874 to 1878 medical practice in New Brunswick

October 1878 minister of public works

1879 knighted by Queen Victoria, as a knight commander in the Order of Saint George and Saint Michael

1879 minister of railways and canals

1881 tour to British Columbia including Victoria and Vancouver

June 1883 High Commissioner to England

March 1887 to May 23, 1888 minister of finance

1888 high commissioner to England

September 12, 1888 declared a baron by Queen Victoria

1896 January appointed secretary of state

May 1, became prime minister of Canada on the resignation of Bowell

July 8, resigned as prime minister and conceded the election

1896 – 1901 in Opposition

1901 lost his seat in the election, retired from electoral politics

1902 moved with his wife Frances, their daughter Emma, and granddaughter Marie to live at Bexley Heath in North Kent, England.

1907 appointed member of Britain's Privy Council

1908 tour of western provinces as he retired

1912 death of his wife Frances

1915 October 30, death by heart failure

Bibliography

Blake, Donald E. *Two Political Worlds: Parties and Voting in British Columbia*. Vancouver, BC: UBC Press, 1985. p135.

Brown, Brian M. "Poundmaker, Big Bear, and the 1885 Rebellion." alittlehistory.com Revised 2001. Retrieved April 30, 2016. http://www.alittlehistory.com/NativeRb.htm

Brown, Craig, ed. *Illustrated History of Canada*, 25th anniversary edition. Montréal,QC: McGill-Queen's University Press, 2012.

de Tremaudan, A.-H. *Hold High Your Heads (History of the Metis Nation in Western Canada)*. Trans: Elizabeth Maguet. Winnipeg, MB: Pemmican Publications and L'Union Nationale Métisse St. Joseph du Manitoba, 1982.

"The Honourable Sir Charles Tupper." Canada Info. Web. Retrieved Sept 13, 2014. http://www.craigmarlatt.com/canada/government/tupper.html

Munroe, Susan. "Prime Minister Sir Charles Tupper: A Father of Confederation, Premier of Nova Scotia, and Canadian Prime Minister." *About News*. Web. Posted 2014. Retrieved September 13, 2014.

Saunders, Edward Manning. *The Life and Letters of the Rt Hon Sir Charles Tupper*, vol 1 & 2. 1916. New York, NY: Cassell, 1916.

Shipley, Nan. *The Road to the Forks: A History of the Community of Fort Garry*. Winnipeg, MB: Stovel-Advocate Press, 1970. http://manitobia.ca/resources/books/local_histories/034.pdf

Sprague, D.N. *Canada and the Métis*. Waterloo, ON: Wilfred Laurier University Press, 1988.

Don't miss out!

Visit the website below and you can sign up to receive emails whenever Paula Johanson publishes a new book. There's no charge and no obligation.

https://books2read.com/r/B-A-ZKUK-KXOIB

BOOKS 2 READ

Connecting independent readers to independent writers.

Also by Paula Johanson

Alt-Academic
Woolgathering: Awareness of the Foreign in Published Works About
Cowichan Woolworking
Sanitizer

Prime Ministers of Canada
Pierre Elliott Trudeau: Child of Nature
Charles Tupper: Warhorse

Slice of Life
No Parent Is An Island
Working Parent
Under The Plow

Young Science
Bat Poop Sparkles
Otters Hold Hands

Standalone

Small Rain and Other Nightmares
Island Views
Plum Tree
Tower in the Crooked Wood
King Kwong: Larry Kwong, the China Clipper Who Broke the NHL Colour
Barrier
Science Critters
Green Paddler

Watch for more at books2read.com/paulaj.

About the Author

Paula Johanson is a Canadian writer. A graduate of the University of Victoria with an MA in Canadian literature, she has worked as a security guard, a short order cook, a teacher, newspaper writer, and more. As well as editing books and teaching materials, she has run an organic-method small farm with her spouse, raised gifted twins, and cleaned university dormitories. In addition to novels and stories, she is the author of forty-two books written for educational publishers, among them *The Paleolithic Revolution* and *Women Writers* from the series *Defying Convention: Women Who Changed The World*. Johanson is an active member of SF Canada, the national association of science fiction and fantasy authors.

Read more at books2read.com/paulaj.

About the Publisher

Doublejoy Books is the publisher of a variety of eclectic books of Canadian literature.

http://doublejoybooks.com
http://books2read.com/paulaj